What people are saying about
Overcoming Life's Challenges

"I have greatly enjoyed working through Steve Baird's *Overcoming Life's Challenges* with my men's small group. We found the book to be insightful and helpful in guiding our examination of the scriptural basis for the trials in our lives. I heartily recommend this book both for personal study and for small group use."

Kelly Walter | Founding Pastor | Rock Brook Church

"I want to personally recommend to you, *Overcoming Life's Challenges*, an engaging and enlightening look at chapter one of the epistle of James. Steve has given real insight and application to a unilateral problem that we all face, how can we overcome the harsh reality of heartache, disappointment, and discouragement? How is joy possible in the midst of our struggles? How can I glorify God in this trial? I encourage you to take the time and read this book, and I'm confident you will reap the benefits."

Dr. Steve Dighton | Pastor Emeritus | Lenexa Baptist Church

"This tome by Steve Baird does not flow from some personal tragedy and as a consequence have limited application; rather his careful exegesis of James 1:1-12 unlocks timeless principles from which anyone may benefit. What I know of his personal life puts added punctuation to that previous comment. Any study group would greatly benefit from a close perusal of this book."

Stanley V. Udd, ThD | Retired Professor of Biblical Languages

"Sports are a microcosm of life, and the Christian athlete can learn much from the trials that regularly show up because of competition. My friend and college basketball teammate, Steve Baird, has persevered through enough of those challenges to complete this quality 'assignment.' I can't think of anyone who would not benefit from reading this book."

John M. Conway | Field Associate | Fellowship of Christian Athletes

"Steve does a great job in this book of explaining biblical principles in a practical, common sense way. Anyone can benefit from reading this book. I highly recommend it."

Dana Jermain | Partner | Deloitte

OVERCOMING LIFE'S CHALLENGES

Do I Need to Know This for the Final?

James 1:1-12

By Steve Baird

OVERCOMING LIFE'S CHALLENGES
Do I Need to Know This for the Final?

DEDICATION

This book is gratefully and lovingly dedicated
to my wife, Lisa.

We have overcome life's challenges together
for 30 years.

I said, "If you marry me,
life will never be boring!"

We could use a little boring!

CONTENTS

A NOTE FROM A FELLOW BEGGAR

Thank you for joining me on the journey to *Overcoming Life's Challenges.* I pray God will use the pages of this book in each of our lives, just as He desires. Before you read each chapter, please ask God to make your ear attentive to heaven. Highlight what God wants you to remember. Put a question mark by something that doesn't make sense or where you are not sure you agree. As you go through your day, let God's Word and principles simmer in the crock-pot of your heart and mind until they are consumed into the core of your being.

At the end of each chapter are questions to point you to the morsel of bread Jesus has for you to ingest in your time of trials. Feast on all the questions as you answer them. Let your palate savor one of the questions. Throw out the distasteful questions. Create your own tasty question or allow the meat God has given you to marinade. Remember, Jesus will meet you at the point of your need - don't miss Him!

As sojourners on this sod, share what God is teaching you, encourage others in the trials of life, let plaguing questions lead you to the Bread of Life, laugh, maybe cry, but realize we are all beggars helping each other find bread.

Several years ago I took a college course in which I was given an assignment to write a paper on "My Philosophy of Christian Education." One of the requirements of the paper was to include an "apology." It was not because my paper would be lame, though that may have been true. It was an apology to the reader because in the area of philosophy, one is always learning, developing, and applying it. A few years down the road, I should grow in my understanding and application of philosophy. The same is true with the writing of this book about life's challenges. Please forgive me for where I fail to live out the principles and words I have written. A few miles down the road, hopefully I will understand and apply the principles better than today. I do believe them deeply and strive to be Christ-like. But, I am one beggar showing another beggar where to find bread. Please take some of the bread God has given me, partake of it, and pass it on.

> "The encourager, no matter how dare the day, always brings a message of hope. Those who encourage… are in effect only beggars telling other beggars where to find help."
>
> -Derick Bingham
> *Encouragement – Oxygen for the Soul*[1]

Introduction

NEXT EXIT:

THE SCHOOL
OF
HARD KNOCKS

"The Christian life is not perfection;
it is a direction."

Welcome to Statistics 101

Each of us have thoughts that agonize our minds, situations that incite our emotions, and events that bring disorder in our lives. They steal our joy, rob our sleep, and deteriorate our health. There are questions begging for answers by plaguing our days and haunting our nights. Questions like: What were the chances of me being born with 11 fingers or toes? What are the odds of me getting the flu this year? Maybe, you find your mind is racing with the possibility of being killed by lightning or bowling a perfect game. Perhaps, you are preoccupied about your odds of becoming the President of the United States of America or achieving the status of billionaire. As you notice the lights on in your neighbor's house, do your thoughts gravitate to that all-important question: what does my neighbor have in his freezer? These particular issues may not interrupt the activities of your day or create a restless night's sleep, but we all have challenges that do. Before we inspect those challenges more closely, here are a few statistics to feed the appetite of curiosity.

> ➤ The odds of being born with 11 fingers or toes are 1 in 500.[1]
> ➤ The odds of getting the flu this year are 1 in 10.[2]
> ➤ The odds of bowling a 300 game are 1 in 11,500.[#]
> ➤ The odds of becoming President of the U.S. are 1 in 10 million.[*]
> ➤ The odds of an American home having at least one container of ice cream in the freezer are 9 in 10.[#]

When we think about the odds of something happening to us personally, we generally talk about the possibilities of being hit by lightning, being attacked by a shark, or winning the lottery. Here are a few statistics about those events:

> The odds of getting attacked by a shark are 1 in 11.5 million.*
> The odds of being killed by lightning are 1 in 2,320,000.#
> The odds of dying in an airplane crash are 1 in 205,532.*

In case those statistics don't give you enough to ruminate about, let the following invade your peace of mind.

> If you want to play in the NBA, the odds of being drafted by the NBA are 1 are 6,864,000.*
> If you want to become a billionaire, the odds are slim to none.*

Statistics are a collection of information given to assist us in understanding, evaluating, or quantifying a particular area. They can be informative or inaccurate. They can be helpful or misleading. They can be up-to-date or out-of-date. They can be interesting or boring. They might even change as some of the ones cited have. The above statistics may not directly impact our lives but there is one statistic that invades each of our lives. It may not be about an extra toe or being hit by lightning or running for President. But without a doubt, it agonizes our minds, incites our emotions, and wreaks havoc on our lives. It causes us to be awake and troubled at night and be tired and grumpy during the day. This statistic is accurate, helpful, up-to-date, and relevant to each one of us.

> # The odds that you and I will experience tests in life are 1 in 1:
> ## →That's 100%!!←

We all experience tests of one kind or another. We have tests in school, driver's tests, aptitude tests, pregnancy tests, blood tests, bar exams, NCLEX-RN exams for nursing, the ACT, test to be a certified sports official, and a multitude of other tests. Each of us will experience different kinds of tests but there is one test we all must take. As much as we try to hide from it, avoid it or ignore it, the statistics of life are proven again and again: we cannot dodge this test. In the hard-knock school of life, we all will have to take the test of trials. Daily, we face life's challenges.

Since it is a foregone conclusion that we will experience the test of trials, our minds make a very small but quick leap to "How do I pass the test of trials?" We might also be lead to ask that frequently voiced classroom question: *"Do I need to know this for the final?"* Of course this question often means: I don't want to study or learn anything I don't absolutely need to know in order to pass the final test. In life, we tend to be the same way. We want to skate by with minimum effort in overcoming life's challenges. God, however, is not just interested in our "passing" or "failing". He is committed to developing our faith in a way that it will demonstrate itself in the midst of the most trying of tests. God is actively teaching us what He wants us to learn in order to reflect Jesus' character in every area of our lives. Passing or failing this test does not achieve salvation or favor with God; instead it demonstrates and develops the faith we have in Jesus Christ.

As we embark together on this journey of learning to pass the tests of trials, we find valuable similarities between the tests in the academic setting and the tests in our spiritual life. To draw on this analogy, let us start at the beginning of the school year, where we kick off "Back to the School of Hard Knocks" events. Our events will consist of: Meet the Teacher Night, Preview Day, and Curriculum Night.

Meet the Teacher Night

Before each school year starts our children have a "Meet the Teacher Night." It is a night when each of the students and their parents can go to their respective school and have a meet and greet with their new teacher or teachers for the coming school year. It is a time to begin to build the teacher-pupil relationship. When it comes to the School of Hard Knocks, our Teacher is the Holy Spirit and His text book is the Word of God. As we seek to learn how to pass the test of trials, ask the Holy Spirit to be your Teacher.

> But the Advocate, **the Holy Spirit**, whom the Father will send in my name, **will teach you all things** and will remind you of everything I have said to you (John 14:26).

> But when he, **the Spirit of truth**, comes, **he will guide you into all the truth**. He will not speak on his own; he will speak only what he hears, and he will tell you what is yet to come (John 16:13).

As we meet the Divine Teacher, we are also cognitive of the fact that God the Holy Spirit guided humans to write His Word (cf. 2 Peter 1:20-21). One such man was James, who wrote the book in the New Testament that bears his name. Though the Holy Spirit of God is ultimately our Teacher, He will use James to be our human teacher for our class on trials. Let's take a moment to meet James.[3]

James had the unprecedented privilege of being Jesus' earthly half-brother as we find in Matthew 13:54-56:

> Coming to his [Jesus] hometown, he began teaching the people in their synagogue, and they were amazed. "Where did this man get this wisdom and these miraculous powers?" they asked. "Isn't this the carpenter's son? Isn't his mother's name Mary, and aren't his [Jesus'] brothers **James**, Joseph, Simon and Judas? Aren't all his sisters with us? Where then did this man get all these things?"

Undoubtedly, James was indelibly influenced and impacted by Jesus' life and teachings. Surely James heard Jesus speak on several occasions. Upon close examination, we find James' life and his book deeply reflect Jesus, especially the Sermon on the Mount.

It didn't start that way. James and his family thought Jesus was crazy. Mark 3:21[4] provides us with this insight: *"When his [Jesus'] family heard about this, they went to take charge of him, for they said, 'He [Jesus] is out of his mind.'"* Imagine if your brother stated that He was God and was going to die for the sins of the world, including yours. You too would think His elevator doesn't go all the way to the top. It was probably not until later in his life that James became a believer and follower of Jesus Christ.

James' thinking and his life were radically changed. He had the grand honor of seeing the resurrected Christ.

> For what I received I passed on to you as of first importance: that Christ died for our sins according to the Scriptures, that he was buried, that he was raised on the third day according to the Scriptures, and that he appeared to Cephas, and then to the Twelve. After that, he appeared to more than five hundred of the brothers and sisters at the same time, most of whom are still living, though some have fallen asleep. **Then he [Jesus] appeared to James**, then to all the apostles... (1 Corinthians 15:3-7).

Not only was James' life transformed, but all of our lives are forever altered when we meet and get to know the risen Savior.

James played an intricate role in the early church in Jerusalem. He probably held the position of one of the Pastors, perhaps the Senior Pastor. Some view the book of James as snippets from his sermons. As one of the leaders of the church in Jerusalem, he helped lead a council to determine how the sudden new Gentile believers should be included in the church.

> When we arrived at Jerusalem, the brothers and sisters received us warmly. The next day Paul and the rest of us went to see **James**, and all the elders were present. Paul greeted them and reported in detail what God had done among the Gentiles through his ministry (Acts 21:17-19).

Preview Day

In the years our children moved from elementary school to middle school and from middle school to high school, they participated in a "Preview Day". This happens the day before classes begin. The students go to their new building in order to find their classrooms and start to become acclimated to the changes of a new building, environment, and teachers. The returning students do not attend, and it is very helpful in preparing the new students to adjust to this new phase in their schooling.

As we move from phase to phase in our education about the trials of life, let us move from the building of self to the building of Jesus Christ. It is time we transition from the school of self-handling of trials to the school of Jesus Christ's power to deal with trials. As we acclimate to God's learning environment, we note three truths about Jesus Christ that give us a solid foundation for dealing with life's challenges.

First, Jesus Christ is thoroughly familiar with the lessons He is teaching us, and He is actively committed to enabling us to learn them. Jesus loves us so much that He will not stop His work in our lives until it is finished. The Apostle Paul confirms this by giving us a tremendous promise in this regard: *"being confident of this, that he who began a good work in you will carry it on to completion until the day of Christ Jesus"* (Philippians 1:6). One commentator provides helpful insight, when he says, "...God is so determined to perfect His good work in us that He will continue to do so with whatever it takes, regardless of the obedience or disobedience of the Christian."[6] Jesus' love for us does not wane if we fail a test, nor is it bolstered if we pass a test, but God's resolve is to actively and aggressively accomplish His work in us.

> *"God loves us too much to take anything less than an aggressive role in the development of our character."*
>
> -Gary Mayes, *Now What!*[5]

Second, Jesus promises to go through the test of trials with us. His Word continually reminds us of the fact that we are not alone, but Jesus will be with us! Let the words of the Lord to Isaiah be words of comfort and strength to each of us, as we go through the raging rapids of troubles and the fiery tests of trials.

But now, this is what the Lord says—
he who created you, Jacob,
he who formed you, Israel:
"Do not fear, for I have redeemed you;
I have summoned you by name; you are mine.
When you pass through the waters,
I will be with you;
and when you pass through the rivers,
they will not sweep over you.
When you walk through the fire,
you will not be burned;
the flames will not set you ablaze.
For I am the Lord your God,
the Holy One of Israel, your Savior..."

Isaiah 43:1-3a

Third, Jesus Christ gives us His power to pass the test of trials. *"You, dear children, are from God and have overcome them, because the one who is in you is greater than the one who is in the world"* (1 John 4:4). As we have saving faith in Jesus, He takes up residency within each believer. We have access to the incredible power that raised Him from the dead. Plug into that power as you face the challenges of life.

Curriculum Night

At the beginning of the school year, a curriculum night is also offered. The intent is to communicate to parents and students the material that will be covered in a particular class or subject for the coming school year. It maps out the proposed journey for the course, what landmarks will be passed along the way, and a description of the final destination.

James' message charts out this path for the believer. If we have genuine faith in Jesus Christ, it will be evident by a change in the way we live our lives. The saying, "I can't hear what you're saying because your actions are speaking so loud" is true. I don't have to know what you believe; it will be evident by the way you live. What we really believe will show itself in how we behave. How we behave is indicative of what we believe. The tests that James outlines for us will reveal genuine saving faith. We can derive this from two key passages James gives us in his letter:

> Consider it pure joy, my brothers and sisters, whenever you face trials of many kinds, because you know that **the testing of your faith** produces perseverance (James 1:2-3).

> But someone will say, "You have faith; I have deeds." Show me your faith without deeds, and **I will show you my faith by my deeds** (James 2:18).

This author views the book of James as a series of tests of our faith.[7] James unfolds each test in a way that outlines for us how God would have us respond and grow. These tests are both to demonstrate that our faith is genuine and to develop our faith into a maturity in Christ. In a brief 108 verses, you will find James' writing to be very convicting and very practical.

As we walk along with James, the great sage, he provides milestones of wisdom to continually move us forward in our faith. Our tendency is to look for the easiest and quickest way to pass the tests, so we ask, *"Do I need to know this for the final?"* As our attention is drawn to James' first test, "The Test of Trials", we realize the objective for us is to learn and change from the inside out. It is not just to pass, for how many times have we "passed" a test in school but did not learn the material? Tests, trials, and challenges are unavoidable in our lives; consequently, James gives us six principles as a study guide for:

How to pass the test of trials:

1. We pass the test of trials by **yielding our trials to God's Power**. James 1:1

2. We pass the test of trials by **seeing our trials from God's Perspective**. James 1:2

3. We pass the test of trials by **understanding our trials accomplish God's Purpose**. James 1:3-4

4. We pass the test of trials by **allowing our trials to teach us God's Prayer**. James 1:5-8

5. We pass the test of trials by **letting our trials lead us to God's Place**. James 1:9-11

6. We pass the test of trials by **remembering our trials have God's Promise**. James 1:12

Have I not commanded you? Be strong and courageous. Do not be frightened, and do not be dismayed, for the LORD your God is with you wherever you go.

Joshua 1:9 (ESV)

As we embark on his course *"Overcoming Life's Challenges"*, James' own words give us God's desired outcome: *"Do not merely listen to the word, and so deceive yourselves. Do what it says"* (James 1:22). We have to carefully listen to and examine the Word of God, but if we stop at mere knowledge, we mislead ourselves into thinking we will pass the tests of trials. This is like memorizing the answers to the final in order to pass but not learning the material to the point that it makes a difference in one's life. James emphatically shouts, **"Do what it says!"** In allowing each of these principles to shape us, the result will be a transformed life. This is the difference the testing of our faith is intended to make in each of us.

Conscientiously explore each principle, spend the needed time to hear what God wants you to hear by keeping your ear tuned to His voice, and then commit to doing what God wants you to do. Provided at the end of each chapter is a *"Think About It & Talk About It"* section to guide us in taking each principle from hearing to doing. Focus on one or all of the questions. Come up with your own questions. Think them through. Talk about them with someone else. Wrestle with God in prayer about them. Ask someone to keep you accountable. Ask God to give you the strength not to be only a hearer of His Word but a doer of His Word in the areas where you are facing trials and challenges right now. Remember He promises to go with you through the test of trials.

We started this introduction with statistics, and we will finish with statistics. I used to teach a college course that was basically a *How to Study in College* class. I loved to share the following statistics. I know the percentages are arbitrary, but the point is not.

5% of all college students think.
15% of college students think they think.
80% of college students would rather die than think.

Let's look at it this way: Christians are believers who walk the walk by being doers of the Word.

5% of all believers are doers of the Word.
15% of all believers talk about being doers of the Word.
80% of all believers would rather live for themselves than be doers of the Word.

At this very moment, each of us finds ourselves going into, in the middle of, or coming out of a trial. In the pages to come, as we dissect together these six principles, keep this in mind: The Christian life is not perfection; it is a direction. The heavenly Father is continually at work

You, therefore, will be perfect [growing into spiritual maturity both in mind and character, actively integrating godly values into your daily life], as your heavenly Father is perfect.

Matthew 5:48 (AMP)

to use our tests, trials, and challenges to move us in a direction toward Perfection. That Perfection is Jesus Christ.

A twinge of anxiety or the uneasiness of inadequacy might be raising the hair on the backs of our necks. Why? Because the Christian life is impossible to live on our own, we continually have difficulty moving in the right direction, and we definitely fall short in our attempts to be like Jesus. The good news is that we are all in the same boat rowing against our culture, our sinful desires, and the attacks of the evil one. In chapter one, we will find encouragement and strength to plug into God's power for victory during times of trials and challenges.

If you were put on trial for being a Christian, would there be enough evidence for a jury to convict you?

NEXT EXIT: THE SCHOOL OF HARD KNOCKS

-Think About It & Talk About It-

1. From the beginning of the Introduction, which of the statistics are the most interesting to you? Which are the hardest to believe? What statistics would you be interested in knowing about?

2. Meet the Teacher Night: *"But the Advocate, the Holy Spirit, whom the Father will send in my name, will teach you all things and will remind you of everything I have said to you"* (John 14:26). What does it mean to you personally that the Holy Spirit is ultimately your Teacher in the challenges of life?

3. What did you learn about James? How do you connect with him? Why do you think he is qualified to speak about the test of trials?

4. Philippians 1:6 states, *"being confident of this, that he who began a good work in you will carry it on to completion until the day of Christ Jesus."* What comfort and strength does this verse give you in the midst of life's trials? One commentator stated: "...God is so determined to perfect His good work in us that He will continue to do so with whatever it takes, regardless of the obedience or disobedience of the Christian." What does this comment mean to you?

5. Which of the six principles that will teach us *"How to pass the tests of trials"* are you looking forward to the most? What trials are you facing right now? How can we pray for you and your trials this week?

Chapter 1

MY TEACHER DOESN'T LIKE ME!

Yield Our Trials To God's Power

James 1:1

"Never forget what Jesus did for you. Never take
lightly what it cost Him. And never assume
that if it cost Him His very life,
that it won't also cost you yours."

-Rich Mullins, Musician

English Influenza

As the students straggled into school, their heartbeats quickened and their breaths shortened. An uneasy sensation began to creep, move quickly, and then sprint down their arms until moisture appeared on the palms of their hands. It was the onslaught of the dread disease 8th graders would contract every fall. It was the "English Influenza" or better known as Mrs. Van Sant! She was the teacher every student prayed they would not get but inevitably did. In the world of a young teenager, it seemed like *"in the beginning God created Mrs. Van Sant."* Her hair was a blinding white color. She wore enormous bug-eyed glasses and dresses with high collars and long sleeves. Her voice was like the peal of thunder that rattled the bones and penetrated the souls of her young learners.

Mrs. Van Sant showed no favoritism. She would call students by name to conjugate verbs, quote particles of speech, and drill the rules of grammar into those stubborn, yet impressionable minds. The students were convinced that Mrs. Van Sant did not like them, but she had a deep passion. It was passion for each student to learn grammar. And English grammar, we DID learn!

Mrs. Van Sant was my 8th grade English teacher. At times I was afraid of her, did not like her, and felt she was out to get me, but Mrs. Van Sant was one of the best teachers I ever had. I learned much from her classes, her methods, her character, and her life. As a communicator, I realize her tenacity in teaching English grammar had a lasting impact on me. Any proficiency I have in this area, I am indebted to Mrs. Van Sant.

Though her lessons were difficult and unpleasant, they were not because she did not like me, but because she cared deeply about each of her students. Her passion for us to be prepared for a lifetime of correct English exceeded the enticement to let us be comfortable in her class.

No earthly story will ever completely explain the spiritual, but only serves to cast a sliver of light to see it more clearly. As we seek to understand how God wants us to view and pass the tests of trials, parallels begin to emerge between our teacher and our Lord Jesus Christ. When encountering the testing of our faith, we may feel Jesus is distant, uncaring, or doesn't even like us. As the test unfolds, we may not know or understand what God is teaching us. It is difficult to trust Him. Like the teacher, He knows the material completely and the best way for each of us to learn the eternal lessons. In the end, we realize God cares more about our spiritual maturity than our earthly comfort. He is passionate and actively involved in preparing us to live a life that reflects Jesus Christ.

From the very first verse of James letter, we begin to discover the principles of how to pass the testing of our faith.

James, a servant of God and of the Lord Jesus Christ,   To the twelve tribes scattered among the nations: Greetings.

James 1:1

In James' unusual greeting[1] to his letter, he introduces us to the first principle: **We pass the test of trials by yielding our trials to God's power.** It must be note that as we refer to "unleashing" God's power, it is intended to mean that somehow we control God's ability. An outlet has electricity but if a lamp is not plugged in or turned on the power is not "unleashed". Let's note three bedrock concepts that develop our first principle: God's power is unleashed by surrendering our will, relinquishing our control, and reaching out to our fellow believers.

God's Power is Unleashed Through Us by Surrendering Our Will

A temptation in reading the letters of the New Testament is to quickly leap over the greetings to get to the "meaty" part of the letter. Let us stop to savor James' greeting, for it allows us to sample the flavor of what is to come. This is seen as James starts his letter by saying: *"James, a servant of God"*.

From the ink he put on the very first page, James wants us to know that he is a servant of God. Interestingly, as James originally wrote his letter in the Greek language, he uses a Greek construction[2] that equates himself as a servant. James is saying: **James = slave.** Undoubtedly, today we may struggle with the concept and connotations of a "slave" and may experience many different emotions. Much can be said regarding that issue but for now we will restrict our look at James' usage and context of the word servant. The point James makes by equating himself as a

33

slave is that he has surrendered his life to do the work God has called him in order that God might accomplish His great purpose and write His eternal story.

It is noteworthy that James uses the Greek word *doulos*, which means bond-servant or slave. He did not refer to himself by the often-used Greek word *diakonos*. *Diakonos* means servant or one that waits tables and it is the word from which we get our English word deacon. An understanding of *doulos*, slave, is vital in order to comprehend how James views

> ### KOINE GREEK
>
> *The New Testament was originally written in koine Greek. We will refer to the Greek at times to gain a clearer understanding of James meaning.*
>
> *Koine means common. In the time of James, koine Greek was the language of the common man and used as a trade language, much like English is today.*

himself and challenges us to be overcomers. In this context he presents to us on how to pass the test of trials, *doulos* renders a rich meaning.

This Greek word *doulos* has the idea of an individual who is in debt, i.e. borrowing money from another and becoming a slave in order to pay that debt. It carries more of an employee/employer relationship concept. The employee or slave (*doulos*) works for the employer and the wages earned are a reduction of the debt owed. As we delve into Exodus 21:2-6 we gain a fuller picture of what a bond-servant (*doulos*) meant in the mind of the 1st Century Jew, James' view of his relationship with God, and how James wants us to relate to God in trials.

> If you buy a Hebrew servant, he is to serve you for six years. But in the seventh year, he shall go free, without paying anything. If he comes alone, he is to go free alone; but if he has a wife when he comes, she is to go with him. If his master gives him a wife and she bears him sons or daughters, the woman and her children shall belong to her master, and only the man shall go free. But if the servant declares, "I love my master and my wife and children and do not want to go free," then his master must take him before the judges. He shall take him to the door or the doorpost and pierce his ear with an awl. **Then he will be his servant for life** (Exodus 21:2-6).

The Old Testament law would not allow for the exploitation of fellow Hebrew slaves, so every seven years the slave must be allowed to go free. The slave serving the employer could fall in love with the boss and the situation. In essence, the slave would say, "Master (boss) you have treated me so well, I don't want to leave." The bond-servant could voluntarily decide to take a piercing of the ear which would be a "branding" mark. This mark would boldly make the statement, "I'm yours for life by choice." James is saying this is what he has done and by implication for you and me to do this also. The very first step we take in the test of trials is to say: **"I am making a lifetime commitment to serve Jesus Christ."**[3]

The camp was nestled deep in the heart of the Ozarks. The meeting area consisted of a concrete slab, huge metal support beams, and a metal roof. Whenever the rain traveled through, it pounded against the metal roof drowning out the speaker. Running behind the meeting slab, were train tracks. Whenever the train chucked by, its clickety-clack is all that could be heard. Many speakers would give way to the noise by having the campers count the cars. The sweltering summer nights would invade the meeting area without mercy. In the midst of all this, I made one of the most important decisions of my life. I felt God calling me into full-time ministry. As I talked with a counselor, he gave me one of the best pieces of advice I have ever received. He used 1 Corinthians 6:19-20 to explain to me that I was not surrendering to the ministry but

> Do you not know that your bodies are temples of the Holy Spirit, who is in you, whom you have received from God? You are not your own; you were bought at a price. Therefore honor God with your bodies.
>
> 1 Corinthians 6:19-20

acknowledging the fact that my life already belongs to Jesus. I was committing myself to Him to use anyway He wanted. That night, I made a lifetime commitment to serve Jesus Christ.

James' first words of his letter reflect his style. He is known to be right in our face, step on our toes, and penetrate our hearts. For us to begin to deal with trials in our lives, we must grapple with this concept of a Christian slave and be willing to surrender to the Father, however, this chafes at the very core of our being. We do not want anyone to be over us, tell us what to do, or give up our will. If we're honest, this includes God. But this is where James begins and where we begin to pass the test of trials. **It is a lifetime commitment.**

Nowhere is this better seen than the epic battle between Satan and God. Satan was an extraordinary creation of God. Though he was the highest created angel and had a tremendous role of God's chief worship leader, he was not content with his position. To Satan it was too subservient, so he boldly and proudly proclaimed, *"I will make myself like the Most High"* (Isaiah 14:14b). At a minimum, he wanted to be equal with God and not under Him or surrender his will. Though we would never want to say this out loud, when we fight for our own will, we are following Satan's example, and this is one of Satan's chief goals.

In stark contrast is the surrendered life Jesus modeled for us while on earth. On the Mount of Olives, in the Garden of Gethsemane, Jesus prayed, *"Father, if you are willing, take this cup from me; yet not my will, but yours be done"* (Luke 22:42). Many of us have heard these words of Christ often and we do not give careful consideration to them. Let's think of them as though hearing them for the first time.

SATAN'S "I WILL" PROCLAIMATIONS

You said in your heart,
"**I will** ascend to the heavens;

I will raise my throne
above the stars of God;

I will sit enthroned on the mount
of assembly, on the utmost
heights of Mount Zaphon.

I will ascend above
the tops of the clouds;

I will make myself like
the Most High."

Isaiah 14:13-14

With the coolness and darkness of the night closing in on the garden, Jesus encountered trials and in that moment He let us see He relates to each of us. Jesus and his Father had planned this very moment in history from before the clock of time began to tick, but now Jesus asked the Father, "Was there another plan?" Jesus was not rebelling against the Father, like Satan had. As God, Jesus knew what the very next day would hold. He would hang on a Roman cross taking an eternity's worth of punishment to pay for our sins. In His humanity, Jesus' would agonize but the power of God enabled Him to pray "not my will but thine, be done". It will not be easy to get to a place where we can wear a name tag that says, "Hello, my name is SLAVE."

As James' life calls us to commit ourselves to God and utilize His power, it also challenges us to think deeply about being God's slave. Our concept of a slave (or servant) is to report to the master, make a list of tasks, and go accomplish them with our own strength and resolve. As Henry Blackaby discusses in his book *Experiencing God,* we have it all wrong. Christ left the Holy Spirit to reside in the believer, so we do not need to try harder to serve God but give more control of ourselves to the Holy Spirit to complete the work God has for us to do. "Being a servant of God is different from being a servant of a human master. A servant of a human master works *for* his master. God, however, works *through* His servants."[4]

"The mark of a saint is not perfection, but consecration. A saint is not a man without faults, but a man who has given himself without reserve to God."

Brooke Foss Westcott, Greek Scholar

We are like a lamp that is not plugged into the outlet. The lamp does not give light, but that has nothing to do with the power of the electricity. We must be quick to note that God is powerful regardless of whether we are plugged into Him or yield to Him. But by surrendering our will to God, we plug into God's power and it flows through us. It is "unleashed." It is only when we stop saying, "I will be like the Most High" and start saying, "Not my will but yours be done" that God's power is set free to work in and through us. For the Christian, victory comes through surrender!

God's Power is Unleashed Through Us by Relinquishing Our Control

We are all control freaks! We want to control our spouses, children, health, co-workers, the traffic, the weather, our money, our favorite sports teams, the breakdown of our vehicles, our problems, our trials, our lives, and even God. Yes, each one of us want to control certain areas in our lives and when we cannot, we become angry, depressed, withdrawn, addicts, or myriad of other self-defeating thoughts and activities. The reality is there are very few things we are really in control of - scary thought!

My third of three sons just received his driver's license. Again, I am reminded that I am much more comfortable when I am driving than when I am a passenger. When he (or anyone else) is driving, I'm not in control. As our neighbors are out for a casual stroll, my son is completely comfortable that we are not going to drive onto the sidewalk to hit and mane them, but I am not. I feel compelled to tell him (okay, yell): "Slow down!" "Don't take such wide turns at the corners!" I am not at the wheel. I am not in control and there is really not much I can do. I am freaked out!

We want to control God too! After all God is in control of all things and if we can control Him, we can control our trials and challenges that come our way. He is in control of trials and we are not, that is one reason they are difficult for us. He allows and dictates where, when, how, by whom, what kind, and why, trials are in our lives. We are not in the driver's seat. We are not comfortable. The idea of God being in control can bring comfort to us at times but to relinquish our control to Him, freaks us out!

As James' opening greeting continues to unfold, we observe he also describes himself as, *"a servant of the Lord Jesus Christ"*. We might have the temptation to name drop, but James does not. He does not say, "Hey, I have something to say and a valid platform to say it because Jesus Christ is my half-brother." "You know Jesus, my half-brother, I saw Him after He came back from the dead, so I have a special privilege and the right to speak to you." James identifies Jesus Christ is his Lord. James has accepted and given him the control of his life. James is not freaked out!

Just like us, this is something James had to learn. James was at a point in his life where he let

> *"People want the front of the bus, the back of the church, and the center of attention."*
>
> -Unknown

go of the controls thus plugging into God's power and allowing it to be released through him. Not only does James calls Jesus Lord, so do we. We love to say and sing that Jesus is the Lord of lords but when it comes down to it, we do not really want Him to be Lord over OUR lives. We enjoy speaking of Jesus' sovereignty and that He will reign forever as King of Kings but we don't want Him to sit on the throne of our lives and be OUR King. We brag about the fact that

Jesus has all things in His control, but Jesus better not try to control our lives and definitely not our trials unless He is handling them the way we want. We long for that day when all those pagans, derelicts, degenerates, jerks, idiots, spouses, bosses, neighbors, athletes, actors, musicians, politicians will *"at the name of Jesus bow their knee"* and *"their tongues declare that Jesus Christ is Lord to the glory of God the Father"* (see Philippians 2:9-11). There is one person we don't include in that list, that one person looks back at us in the mirror. We struggle with bowing the knee of our heart before the Lord Jesus and using our tongue to declare Jesus as Lord, because when we do, we are clearly saying we are not in control.

At one point, James too was a control freak. James thought he was behind the wheel, fully in control of steering his own course in life. Something changed along the way. James finally got it when he let go of the controls! Jesus was not his insane, never-do-anything-wrong brother but His Lord, His Messiah, the risen One. Jesus died for James' sin. James had the unbelievable privilege of seeing the resurrected Christ and was never the same. By genuinely seeing and meeting the risen Savior, each of us will allow our hands to loosen our grip on the steering wheel of our lives and place it in the nail-scarred hands.

By identifying Jesus as Lord, James is handing over the controls of his life to risen Savior. Who has control over life and death? Only God! The Apostle Paul, who also saw the risen Savior, puts it this way; *"I also pray that you will understand the incredible greatness of God's power for us who believe him. This is the same mighty power that raised Christ from the dead and seated him in the place of honor at God's right hand in the heavenly realms"* (Ephesians 1:19-20 NLT). As we relinquish the steering wheel of our lives to Jesus Christ, that same resurrection power enables us to overcome life's challenges. Are you freaked out to give Jesus the control? Good, because we are all in the same car together!

As we ponder the reality of Jesus Christ as Lord, it means He is sovereign, the King, all powerful, has control of all things, has authority, has made and holds all things together but it also means Jesus does as He pleases. Let the following passages soak into the fabric of your being to the point that they leave a lasting imprint.

> Our God is in heaven; he does whatever **pleases** him (Psalm 115:3).

> The Lord does whatever **pleases** him, in the heavens and on the earth, in the seas and all their depths (Psalm 135:6).

> But he [God] stands alone, and who can oppose him? He does whatever he **pleases** (Job 23:13).

For us, this characteristic of Jesus Christ can be a bit like petting a cat. When we pet a cat in the direction of its fur, it purrs but when we rub the cat against the direction of its fur, it hisses. When God does as He pleases and we like it, we purr with His praises but when God does as He pleases and we don't like it, we hiss at Him in anger, depression, or unfaithfulness. Jesus is not selfish, egotistical, or out for Himself. He simply is acting according to who He is: Jesus is God, the uncreated Creator. The creator of anything has the right to do with his creation as he pleases. I have a friend who writes songs. He puts it this way: "I am the creator of the song. If I want the verse before the chorus or the chorus before the verse, I can do as I please with the song because I am the creator." The same is true of our God. The greatness of our Creator is He carries out His plans and purposes. He allows us to be a part of His never-ending story. This is the message throughout the Scriptures. God wants us to accept who He is and who we are created to be. God brings trials along the pathways of our life to prepare, sharpen, mold, and empower us for the work He is doing and to tell the story He is writing.

In this instance, Jesus is like the teacher because we may not like the fact that He is the Controller of the classroom of our lives and the Master of the material or trials that come our way. Many times, His methods, His purposes, or why He continually pushes us is hard to comprehend, but Jesus does as He pleases to develop His creations as He desires to accomplish His purpose. When we allow Jesus to change us from "Controlled by Self" to "Controlled by Christ", God's enabling power flows through us.

Through this one word "Lord", we have a powerful lesson to learn from James. As we yield our trials to God by relinquishing our control, God's power is available to live in and through us.

God's Power is Unleashed Through Us by Reaching Out to Our Fellow Believers

As we draw our attention again to James' greeting, let us take a moment to savor one more tasty morsel that is embedded in the heart of James, *"To the twelve tribes scattered among the nations: Greetings."* The recipients of James letter were Jewish Christians living outside of Israel and well acquainted with trials, tests, and troubles. They had been dispersed[5] or scattered from their homeland because of the persecution that broke out against the Christian Church in Jerusalem with Saul of Tarsus being the main instigator. God used this scattering to spread the gospel of Jesus Christ. James knew they could become weary in battling trials, so he gives insight and encouragement to them and us.

Beginning In verse two, James transitions from referring to his readers as "the twelve tribes" and begins to refer to his readers as "brothers and sisters". Eighteen times in his brief correspondence, James heart of compassion speaks directly to his brothers and sisters and to us. Throughout the pages of his book, James straightforward and pulls no punches style is sprinkled with the seasoning of tenderness. His words make the message palatable because they leave the aftertaste of: "We're in this together!"

**King Solomon:
The wisest man to ever live**

What has been will be again, what has been done will be done again; there is nothing new under the sun.

Ecclesiastes 1:9

Often we think we don't relate to the men and women of the Scriptures. They seem like superheroes that call on their super powers to thwart off the onslaught of sin and evil. Only an occasional kryptonite trips them up. We often feel other believers have a much better understanding and handle on God, the spiritual journey, and trials. We feel our trials are much harder than theirs and we are more spiritually anemic. We may think, "God is harder on me, incessantly testing me in areas I am weak, or distant and uncaring about me." Some reading these words are questioning God's involvement in his or her life. If God is in "control" and the "master", why doesn't He do something about my pain and trouble? He might even appear to laugh at your trials and dream up problems to make your life miserable. Let's be honest with ourselves, we've all had these thoughts and questions but we are not alone.

Even the men and women of the Scriptures had these intrusive doubt monsters. Questioning God, His character, and His motives places each of us right beside Adam and Eve in Garden of Eden. Genesis 3:1 describes it this way, *"Now the serpent was more crafty than any of the wild animals the Lord God had made. He said to the woman, "**Did God really say**, 'You must not eat from any tree in the garden'?"* Satan used the serpent to cause Adam and Eve to question and doubt God's word and His goodness. God desired Adam and Eve (and us) to live life as He designed it. The result of them thinking "Hey, God is holding out on us by not letting us eat of the fruit of this one tree," began a downward progression.

Satan's Subtle Deceit

But I am afraid that, as the serpent deceived Eve by his craftiness, your minds will be led astray from the simplicity and purity of devotion to Christ.

2 Corinthians 11:3 (NASB)

It led to sin entering into humanity, being exiled from the Garden of Eden and God's presence, and our need for a Savior. This is why

James address, "brothers and sisters" and by extension, you and me. Starting with Adam and Eve throughout history, we all have our doubts, struggles, and challenges. Because we are in this together, we need to reach out to fellow believers.

We may be so self-absorbed or hurt or angry or you fill in the blank, that we won't allow God His rightful place in the universe or the world, much less our lives. We place ourselves or something else in the center of our little universe. We must not allow our thinking to be clouded as Adam and Eve's was. As we draw on the Word of God and trust in God, we begin to gain perspective, God's perspective.

During my graduate work, I studied for three weeks in Israel. When I came home I started reading in Genesis to see in Scripture some of the places I had visited. As I read, I began to observe that the fathers of our faith, Abraham, Isaac, Jacob, and others all did some horrible things. I become disillusioned. I asked my Dad, "Why would God pick these men to be His chosen nation, Israel, and the fathers of our faith? I would never pick them. They were wretches!" With much wisdom, my Dad stated one of the greatest bits of wisdom he has ever given me, "I don't know." But then he continued, "All I know is that God chooses to work through sinful man."

Many of these wretches of the Old Testament are described in Hebrews 11 as men and women of faith. If they can be described as men and women of faith, there is hope for each of us! The point is we draw encouragement from the men and women of Scripture who have gone before us to pass and fail the test of trials and then their lives reach out in encouragement to those of us who come behind. Later in his letter, James makes this connection of commonality between us and the individuals in the Bible; *"Elijah was a human being, even as we are. He prayed earnestly that it would not rain, and it did not rain on the land for three and a half years"* (James 5:17).

Just as James allows God's power to extend from his life and words to reach out to fellow believers, we are challenged to do the same. We can be a conduit for God's power to others, because every believer through all of history and every believer all over the world today faces the same trials we do. The trials that you have may not be particularly hard for me but the ones that easily trip me up may not be a problem for you. The only difference in the trials we experience or the trials in biblical times or the trials in the Philippines or in Zimbabwe or in Amsterdam is the packaging. In his letter, Peter communicates to us we are not alone in this spiritual battle, *"Resist him [Satan], standing firm in the faith, because you know that the family of believers throughout the world is undergoing the same kind of sufferings"* (1 Peter 5:9).

> **A Father's Wisdom**
>
> *"I don't know."*
>
> *"All I know is that God chooses to work through sinful man."*
>
> -Dorrell Baird

Without question James' life itself tells of a man who once thought of Jesus Christ as a lunatic, but now clearly proclaims Jesus is as his Master and Lord. His description of himself humbly communicates that James had surrendered his will and relinquished his control to Jesus Christ. As James reaches out to minister to others going through trials, he is practices what he preaches and challenges us to do the same when he wrote, *"If you really keep the royal law found in Scripture, 'Love your neighbor as yourself.' you are doing right"* (James 2:8).

A.W. Tozer put it this way, "It is doubtful whether God can bless a man greatly until He has hurt him deeply."[6] Why, you may ask? Because, *"Praise be to the God and Father of our Lord Jesus Christ, the Father of Compassion and the God of all comfort, who comforts us in all our troubles, so that we can comfort those in any trouble with the comfort we ourselves have received from God"* (2 Corinthians 1:3-4).

Jesus is Lord in the Fire![7]

James' own words and life throw down the gauntlet for us to pass the test of trials by yielding our trials to God's power. God's power is unleashed through us as we surrender our will, relinquish our control, and reach out to others. During the Reformation we find another, who yielded his trials to God. His life exhibited surrender to doing God's will that brought a monumental trial of being burned at the stake. He relinquished his control to God and in so doing reached out and encouraged his friends in their trials. Let his life be an example of what James is instructing us and a model of what it means to let Jesus Christ be the Master and Controller of our life.

Because of his convictions, Thomas Haukes[8] fearlessly took a stand against the Church of England. His strong belief in following the Word of God over man's traditions led him into a fiery test of his faith. Haukes would not recant his position, so he and six others were declared heretics and sentenced to be burned at the stake on the 9th of February, 1555.

Just before his death, Haukes' friends visited him and expressed they were terrified by the fatality of the punishment staring Thomas in the face. As their time together was ending, his friends questioned whether it was worth paying the price of death for the Lord Jesus Christ and for one's convictions. They specifically asked that in the midst of the flames, Haukes would show them a sign. A gesture to say it was worth the anguish and that one could possess calmness and composure in the center of an extreme trial. Thomas promised his comrades he would do this. It was agreed that if the rage of the pain might be suffered, then before the fire took his life, he would lift up his hands above his head towards heaven.

The time came for Thomas Haukes to be led to the stake where a crowd of curious onlookers had gathered. Just before he was bound, one last time Haukes was asked to renounce his conviction and agree with the Church of England. Knowing his answer would seal his fate; Thomas did not waver and stated he would not recant! With a strong chain placed around his midsection, he was quickly tied to the stake. The wood was lit. This was the beginning of the end of Thomas Haukes' life on earth.

A spark of fire ignited the sticks around his feet. Quickly, the wood turned into a blazing inferno that began to engulf Thomas. The scorching flames did their intended work on Thomas Haukes. His hair was gone and now his fingers burnt off. As the heat of the fire reach Haukes' ears, they too fell off in the fire. His appearance was beyond recognition and his body slumped as life was leaving

Haukes. His friends could hardly look but they waited to see if there would be a sign. A sign, that in dying it was worth living for the Lord Jesus Christ. Thomas Haukes being mindful of his promise reached the charred nubs of what use to be his hands over his head toward God. He struck them together once, twice, three times. A great shout from the crowd followed this unbelievable moment. That unforgettable day was June 10, 1555, when Thomas Haukes would take his last breath and sink into the fire but forever declare,

"Jesus is Lord in the fire!"

Thomas Haukes' life is an inspiration to us to die for our faith but more importantly to live for our Lord Jesus Christ. We might ask ourselves if we could do what he did. Haukes had an unimaginable perspective of God while he was in the thick of his trials. We may not face the same trials Thomas Haukes encountered, but to us, our trials are just as fiery and painful. James will now guide us to see our trials from God's perspective, so we will pass the test in the heat of our trials.

MY TEACHER DOESN'T LIKE ME!
Yield Our Trials to God's Power; James 1:1

-Think About It & Talk About It-

1. Describe your "Mrs. Van Sant". In what ways do you think a teacher helps us relate to God as He gives us the test of trials? In what ways do you think God is different than a school teacher when it comes to the test of trials?

2. What mental pictures come to your mind when you think of a slave? Compare and contrast your mental pictures with the view of a slave described in this chapter? How has James challenged your thinking about what it means to be a "slave" (*doulos*) of Jesus Christ?

3. What area(s) are you a "control freak"? When we talk about God being sovereign or in control, what is most comforting about that? What is most unsettling about that?

4. In what ways have been able to encourage others by your trials and challenges?

5. What are the thoughts that come to your mind when you read the story of Thomas Haukes? How might his life be an encouragement to live out the principles of this chapter?

Chapter 2

BUT I EXPERIENCE TEST ANXIETY!

See Our Trials From God's Perspective

James 1:2

"Top-down thinking begins with God and looks at circumstance. Bottom-up thinking begins with circumstance and may or may not consider God into the equation."

-Mike Grubbs
Top-Down Thinking in a Bottom-up World[1]

The Stress of Tests

Test anxiety is real! I've seen it and I've experienced it, both as a student and as an instructor. When I taught at a Bible College, I worked closely with the director of the Learning Center. Because of their unique challenges and struggles with academics, some students experience extreme test anxiety. I began to understand these students' need for special arrangements for testing. Although many of us may not need assistance or special consideration in testing, we still might experience some elements of test anxiety as described by *The Princeton Review* website.

*While it's completely normal to feel a bit nervous before a test, some students find test anxiety debilitating. Racing thoughts, inability to concentrate, or feelings of dread can combine with physical symptoms like a fast heartbeat, headache, or nausea. Whether it's the **ACT**, an **AP exam**, or an important history final, test anxiety has the power to derail weeks and months of hard work. According to the **ADAA**, causes of test anxiety may include a fear of failure, lack of adequate prep time, or bad experiences taking tests in the past. You're not alone![2]*

For many students, just the mention of "tests" created an uncomfortable feeling, like a pebble in one's shoe. The fear of failure, inadequacy, not measuring up, and other self-defeating thoughts creep in, plaguing the mind with varying degrees of test anxiety. As I administered a test to my class, I would watch with interest as the students who had not studied much would have the "deer in the headlights" look good students would frantically cram up to the last possible second. This scenario would play out time and again, even though I gave them a study guide to help ensure the passing of the test. Typically, testing and some form of anxiety go hand and hand, but there are always a few exceptions, like my friend Barry, who likes to take tests. Most of us look at those individuals like they have a third eye in the middle of their foreheads.

On this journey we call life; I would venture to say that each one of us currently has at least one trial, test, struggle, or challenge that invades us to create feelings of anxiousness. Feelings can leech onto us and are not easy to shake loose. Let's take note of different arenas where we may experience testing. We can easily identify with mental testing. The stress of the test may embed itself in the high school senior needing a good grade to pass a required class, a lawyer-to-be studying to pass the bar examination, or the sixteen-year-old taking a driver's test. A serious illness may threaten our quality of life, or an injury that potentially limits our ability to function as we once did, can bring physical testing. Hospital stays, physical therapy, and financial woes can add more anxiety to physical testing. Depression, fears, anxieties, anger, loneliness, bitterness, and a plethora of other emotions may feel like a wave of the ocean, so big and strong that they leave us gulping for emotional air. These emotional waves of testing might crash in on us, as we lose a loved one or a job. The wave of depression might pound against us as we fail at an endeavour or the wave of anger might try to pull us under as we feel wronged. Relational tests can create many long, uneasy, sleepless nights. We may face the tests of relationships which have no easy answers and are seemingly irreparable with spouses, family members, friends, neighbours, or co-workers. These relational tests can be some of the most difficult and stressful. When we say that we believe God; and we will live by His Word, or when we step out and make a commitment to God in a particular area of our lives, we can rest assured that we will experience spiritual testing. It is as though God says to us, "Alright, if that's what you say you really believe and you are going to trust Me, and if you are making that commitment, then I will put you in a situation to see if you really mean it." There will be a test to show that your faith is real.

Remember, the purpose of testing in life is the goal of testing in academics. It is a tool by which we prove that we know the material, and it produces growth in that area. Just as I would give my students a study guide to aid them in passing my tests, God gives us His Word and His Spirit to instruct us, to empower us, and to pass each of the tests of life. In reality, missing a question or bombing a test is when we learn the most. God knows just what tests we need in order to take the next step in our walk with Him. Definitely they can bring test anxiety, but our perspective regarding trials will make a difference. Test-loving Barry may still be the oddball, but when we see trials from God's perspective we can have confidence that God is at work. This confidence will alleviate some of the anxiety. Jesus asks us to cast our cares on Him because He is up all night anyway. To that end, James gives us two aspects of God's perspective that enable us to pass the tests. God's perspective gives us joy in our trials. God's perspective gives us acceptance of our trials.

God's Perspective Gives Us Joy in Our Trials.
James 1:2a

Consider it pure joy, my brothers and sisters,…
James 1:2a

As James begins to unveil the painting entitled *Trials*, he reveals something of vital importance; God's perspective. Because of sin, we are wired to look at the tests of life through an earthly, bottom-up lens, instead of a godly, top-down lens. *Having **God's perspective is seeing life the way He sees it and living life from that viewpoint.*** This is also known as wisdom. Perhaps that is why some have said that James' book is the Proverbs of the New Testament.

In verse two, James lifts the corner of the veil, clearly exposing how we are to view trials and tests from God's perspective. We are to "*Consider it,*" and James identifies "it" as trials. By looking closer at the meaning of *consider*, we discover this word carries the idea of "to deem or reckon." I like to use the phrase, *in my mind's eye.* As we look with the eye of our mind, James instructs us to gaze through the lens of God's perspective. This is our worldview or viewpoint.

When I was younger, I remember going to the store and trying on sunglasses. It was fun to put on a pair of yellow sunglasses. Amazingly everything in the store took on a yellow tint. If I put on a pair of blue sunglasses, remarkably everything took on a shade of blue. The color of the lens would not change the store nor its contents, but it dramatically impacted how I looked at the store and what was in it. In our mind's eye, when we look through the lens of God's perspective, it does not change life but rather how we see it. It is not a matter of positive thinking, looking for the silver lining, or ignoring pain, troubles, and difficulties of this earthly life. It is allowing God to tint the view through our mind's eye with the same shade of color He sees life. We all wear a pair of perspective sunglasses, which colors everything in our world. In order to understand and respond to the trials of life as God desires, the sunglasses or lens through which the eye of our minds must look is

God's perspective. James begins by unveiling this critical component of the

Consider = *"in my mind's eye"*

painting of trials: God's perspective starts in our minds.

The word *consider* is written in the Greek middle voice, which means we accomplish the action of the verb ourselves.[3] No one can put on the glasses of God's perspective for anyone else. I can't do it for my wife, my sons, my friends, or you. You can't do it for me. Simply put, each of us has the responsibility to put on God's glasses ourselves in order to look at life from God's perspective. This is why we surrender our will to the Master and relinquish our control to the Lord.

James gives this word *consider* to us in the form of a command. It is not an option, a suggestion, or even a good idea. It is imperative! If we are going to deal with the trials of life the way God wants, we must look through the lens of God's eternal perspective that adds His tint to our circumstances. King Solomon gave us advice that reinforces this command of God's perspective, do it with all you have, and not to look at life through our own lens of perspective. *"Trust in the LORD with all your heart and lean not on your own understanding; in all your ways acknowledge him, and he will make your paths straight"* (Proverbs 3:5-6).

Recently, I went to the store to purchase a pair of sunglasses. I decided to return to my childhood for a moment, though my wife would say I've never left it. I found sunglasses that were yellow, blue, and various other shades. I tried them on to remember how they cast a tint of color on the store and its contents, but to my surprise the sunglasses with colored lens did not give the store a tint of yellow or blue. Sunglasses have progressed over the years and now generally do not add this color shading. At first, I thought this weakened my illustration, however, upon reflection, the analogy is even stronger. As sunglasses have developed, they have eliminated that tint of yellow or shade of blue. We feel as though our ability to see the world and our challenges through God's lens has "developed." In reality, we think we are putting on God's lens when the anti-Christian culture in which we live, the worldviews that bombard us, and the wrong understanding of God that permeate our society make God's tint or perspective less obvious. This is why it is important to spend time with God in His Word so as we look through the eye of our mind we see through God's lens of perspective to discern life as God does.

Not only does God's perspective start in our minds, but it moves eighteen inches downward and penetrates our hearts. Our English translations render verse two as, "Consider it pure joy." As James originally wrote in koine Greek, the first words of his sentence are "pure or all joy." In the Greek language of James' time, the words at the beginning of the sentence carry weight and emphasis. As we put on the glasses of God's perspective, the tint that shades everything we look at in life is joy. The very first word in the sentence is a word that means "all." We would say that this lens of joy is not mixed with anything else. It is pure joy.

Driving down the highway, I have never seen a motorist stranded on the side of the road due to a wreck or car trouble who was jumping up and down with gladness. I have visited numerous individuals in the hospital. Some are agonizing over life and death decisions for a loved one. Others recognize their illness or injury will forever change the quality of life for someone else or themselves. They are not doing cartwheels of happiness down the hallway, but I have seen believers in Christ who have joy, peace, and comfort in spite of these circumstances. God instructs us that as we look at everything the way He does, we will have joy. And not just joy, but all joy. It is a pure, full joy.

We find an incredible example of this kind of joy tucked away in the pages of the Old Testament during the days of Nehemiah. Many Israelites had been taken captive from

The Old Testament book of Nehemiah records this incredible account. The part of the account being discussed is noted in parenthesis. To join Nehemiah on his amazing journey, take time to read his story.

their homeland and now were living in Persia. The Israelites living in Jerusalem had experienced great devastation to their beloved Jerusalem, and to their personal lives. God burdened Nehemiah to return to Jerusalem and rebuild the broken-down walls (Nehemiah 1-2). This was a testing of Nehemiah's faith. Following God's prompting, Nehemiah banded together the Israelites and led them to rebuild the wall. The excitement of the project shortly gave way to opposition and criticism from three enemies: Sanballat, Tobiah and Geshem. They claimed the wall would be so flimsy that a fox jumping on it would make it fall (Nehemiah 4:1-3). For fear of the enemy tearing down what they had built, the workers would take turns standing guard with swords, spears, and bows (Nehemiah 4:13-14). These enemies tried to trick Nehemiah into working with them and tried to drive a stake of fear into the Israelites (Nehemiah 6:1-9). Here comes the understatement of the year: Nehemiah and the Israelite workers were experiencing trials. Isn't this the norm?! The fire to do what God wants is quickly doused with the water of opposition. Many times, these fire fighters against joy are Christians, or those who claim to be Christians. Yes, Christians will hurt us, let us down, and steal our joy, so **never** take your eyes of Jesus because He is the pioneer, author, perfecter, and finisher of our faith.

Our lives resonate with the life of Nehemiah and his fellow countrymen. We have experienced a vision, a burden, an excitement, or a work that God prompts us to undertake and then someone quickly criticizes, says that we can't accomplish it, tears down our work, tries to trip us up, or creates fear in us. We make a commitment to let Jesus be Master and Lord, and yet the trials continue to hit us like the relentless crashing of the waves of the ocean. We question and doubt God until we remember to take the glasses of God's perspective, put them on, and see the circumstances the way God sees them. That lens is the lens of joy, and the shade of color it provides is God's perspective.

As we return to the account of Nehemiah, we find that the wall was completed in an unprecedented 52 days, their enemies lost self-confidence, and experienced fear (Nehemiah 6:15-16). How did Nehemiah and the Israelites accomplish this with trials and opposition all around them? As the wall was finished, the law was read by Ezra, and a great celebration ensued. Here is where we find the key to having God's perspective of joy in the midst of trials. It is to focus on the Lord's strength, not ours. *"Nehemiah said, "Go and enjoy choice food and sweet drinks, and send some to those who have nothing prepared. This day is holy to our Lord. Do not grieve, **for the joy of the Lord is your strength**"* (Nehemiah 8:10).

Also, at the dedication of the wall we are told, *"And on that day they offered great sacrifices, rejoicing because God had given them great joy. The women and children also rejoiced. The sound of rejoicing in Jerusalem could be heard far away"* (Nehemiah 12:43).

> "Not by might nor by power, but by my Spirit," says the LORD Almighty.
>
> Zechariah 4:6b

This is a beautiful example of what James is saying to us. It is not a matter of our mustering up joy or keeping the right or positive attitude. It is the joy from the Lord that gives us strength to weather the storms of life. We look out the eye of our mind through the lens of God's perspective that tints our trials with the color of joy. It is not putting on a fake act that we don't have any problems or feel the hurt of pain. Instead we experience the genuine joy that only comes from the Lord. This kind of pure joy is only found in Him. This gives us real strength in the tests of trials. Many of us, including Christians, bury our heads in the sand to avoid, ignore, hide from, or pretend issues don't exist. We can be genuine about the depth of our feelings and acknowledge the height of our challenges and still find the real, lasting joy we long for in the Lord and His strength. This is the hope our desperate world is seeking. When we have God's perspective in trials, we can be this beacon of hope to those around us.

God's perspective that begins in our minds and reflects joy in our hearts will extend to others. James is desirous of this connection even in the way he writes his first two verses. James' word for *Greetings* in verse one is a form of the word from which we get joy. James is greeting his readers and us with joy and instructing us to have joy right in the middle of our trials. We have noted that James speaks to his readers often with the words 'brothers and sisters". Here in verse two, we find the first of several times James adds the word, "my" to brothers. I can hear the tenderness in James' voice as he addresses "my brothers and sisters". In times of difficulty, James speaks the truth to us, but he seasons it with love. The Christian life is hard. Jesus even told us in this world we will have trouble but added that He has overcome the world (John 16:33), so that we might demonstrate an unusual joy in the trials of life. God's perspective in the way we face the trials of life gives hope to the believer and a call to the unbeliever to come to Christ.

> I have told you all this so that you may have peace in me. Here on earth you will have many trials and sorrows. But take heart, because I have overcome the world.
>
> –Jesus (John 16:33 NLT)

God's Perspective Gives Us Acceptance of Our Trials.   James 1:2b

...whenever you face trials of many kinds....

James 1:2b

Acceptance brings freedom. We have discussed our need to look at trials through the eye of our mind and to put on the God-tinted glasses of His perspective. Now James gives us instructions on how to adjust the lens to clearly bring trials into the same focus that God has. The adjustment needed is acceptance, and that acceptance brings freedom. This acceptance of trials is not a fatalist approach which says life is tossing me aimlessly about like a cork at sea. It is an acceptance of what God is doing and a freedom to allow God's purpose in the trials to emerge. We will delve much deeper with James into God's purpose in trials in verses three and four.

Just as doctors use glasses with smaller lens attached to them to magnify and bring clarity to their work, it is with this kind of precision and close inspection that we now examine how James wants us to understand the word "trials."

The Greek word used by James for trials, in verses 2 and 12, is *peirasmos*.[4] The basic meaning comes from the root (*peir*) which means "test." The general meaning of *peir* is "to try to learn the nature or character of someone or something by submitting such to thorough and extensive testing - 'to test, to examine, to put to test, examination, testing.'"[5] **A simple definition is "a trial is a test."** It is a test to find out the character of someone. When we take this simple definition and allow the lens of magnification to bring it into focus, James' definition of trials and their purpose becomes clear.

> **A trial is a test God uses to prove the genuineness of our faith and to develop our maturity in Jesus Christ.**

Armed with this understanding of trials, let us make the necessary adjustments to our lens in order to accept the trials of life, to experience God's freedom, and to pass the test of trials. James delineates four adjustments needed to bring our trials into focus and to see them clearly from God's perspective.

Adjustment #1: Trials will happen! They are inevitable. James says, "whenever." It is not that trials might come but that they *"will"* come! It is not a pessimistic outlook that "if something can go wrong, it will go wrong." Nor is it an outlook of denial, hoping to pursue life in such a way that we don't experience any difficulties. We are to make the necessary corrections to our lens to recognize that when a trial presents itself, God is at work in our lives.

Adjustment #2: Trials will meet us in the natural pathways of our lives! *"Count it all joy, my brothers, when you meet trials of various kinds"* (James 1:2, ESV). Some translations use the words "face" or "fall" meaning "to encounter; usually of misfortune, robbers, sickness." The literal meaning is that of falling into, usually unexpectedly. We find this same word used in the story of the Good Samaritan where it describes a man traveling on the road between Jerusalem and Jericho. He suddenly encounters robbers who beat him and leave him half dead (Luke 10:30). The

Greek word James uses is a compound word. The commentator Zodhiates guides us in how to use this word to make corrections to our lens in order to see God's perspective: *"Peri means 'around, upon, on the side, and piptoo means 'to fall.' ...* **It is 'to fall around, to fall upon, to fall aside, to fall into or among, or to fall into the midst of anything.'"**[6] Just walking in the natural pathways of life, we will encounter trials around us, upon us, beside us, on us, or in our midst.

Adjustment #3: Trials will come in many sizes, shapes, shades, and degrees! By using the phrase "of many kinds," James is describing the myriad of ways trials will assault us. As go to school, work, the store, the

> *The Greek word used in James 1:2 for "many kinds" is the word from which we get our English term "polka dots."*[7]

gym, hang out with friends, and live with family, we will be splattered with trials that are big and small. We will be sprayed with trials shaped like relational issues, financial struggles, physical maladies, mental challenges, and emotional upheaval. Some of the colors of the trials that pepper us will be light, some dark, and some a mixture. Remember: when you least expect it, expect it.

Adjustment #4: Trials will test our faith! The three adjustments above lead us to this fourth adjustment found in James 1:3, *"because you know that the **testing of your faith** produces perseverance."* Going to the eye doctor is stressful to me. I'm concerned that the doctor will get it wrong, even though he has been trained in this field. I do not like it when the doctor puts that apparatus over my eyes and asks me, "Which lens is clearer, the first or the second?" "Is this one better? Or this one?" Sometimes, I can't tell which one is the best! I think a similar difficulty is true of trials. When we can see the difference in our lens and God's, it is easier to acknowledge an adjustment is needed. At other times, the adjustment is very fine and hard to determine, and we can only trust God as the Great Physician who knows exactly what adjustment is needed for us to see His perspective clearly. Whether the adaptation is small or large, we now have a choice. Will we accept the trial and adjust our lens, recognizing that *all trials are a testing of our faith?* God uses them to develop and prove our faith is genuine.

One Degree Off Course

A valid question would be: "Does this discussion on my perspective of trials really impact how I deal with them?" The following will give us a better grasp of why perspective is important, especially God's perspective of joy and acceptance in our trials.

There is an interesting fact about flying. For every single degree you fly off course, you will miss your target landing spot by 92 feet per mile you fly. This is about one mile off target for every 60 miles flown. If you begin at the equator and fly around the earth, one degree off would land you almost 500 miles off target. Obviously, the longer you travel off course, the further you will be away from the intended destination. For example, a flight from New York's JFK to Los Angeles' LAX off by one degree would put you 40 miles out in the Pacific Ocean. The importance of that one degree could be the difference between making it to an important meeting on time, or using your seat as a flotation device. Cruising along at 30,000 feet, it is hard to realize we may be off by one degree. That's why the instruments must be trusted. Straying off course can happen, and in-flight adjustment along the way must be made.

Seeing trials from God's perspective is like this. If we don't look through our mind's eye with the lens of God's perspective, we get off course. We all get off course from time to time but the longer we are "one degree" off from God's viewpoint of life and trials, the more we will struggle with challenges, resent God, and fail the tests of trials. Each one of us must continually monitor and make changes to our life's course. When the pilot can't discern his way, he must trust his instruments to keep him on course. In the same way, when we are unsure of what to do in life's trials, we must trust the instrument of God's Word to show us when we are straying off course. With God's grace, be determined to put on God's glasses to see as He sees and make adjustments to your lens by bringing your life into the clear focus of God's perspective. **You won't regret it!**

Perspective makes me think of those pictures that are really, really close to an object, such as an orange, a nail, a dress shoe, or a tennis ball. As you look at a close-up photo of the object, you try to guess what the item is. The next picture is shown from a distance, and you get perspective to see clearly what the object is. James has given us the picture that enables us to step back and gain God's perspective on trials; however, as we look at the picture another question now sneaks in and begins to consume our thoughts. What is God's purpose for allowing or bringing trials into our lives?

BUT I EXPERIENCE TEST ANXIETY!

Seeing our Trials from God's Perspective; James 1:2

-Think About It & Talk About It-

> *Think of the last flight you were on. Where would you have ended up if the pilot was **"one degree off"**?*

1. What makes you anxious? Why do you think that is? Right now, which test(s) are you experiencing: mental, physical, emotional, relational, or spiritual? How would you describe your emotional state in each of those tests of trials?

2. If someone asked you how a Christian can have real joy in trials, what would you tell him/her? How do some people display "fake joy" in their times of trials? What is the difference between real (or pure) joy and fake joy?

3. How does the illustration of the tinted sunglasses help you understand seeing life, especially trials, from God's perspective? Take one challenge you are experiencing, put on God's glasses of perspective, and describe how you will look at that challenge.

4. Our definition for trials derived from James is: *A trial is a test God uses to prove the genuineness of our faith and to develop our maturity in Jesus Christ.* In this chapter, we focused on *"A trial is a test God uses..."* How does the Greek word James used for trial help us understand them? From James 1:2, what are three observations you can make about trials?

5. Four adjustments were noted to help you focus your trials from God's perspective. Which adjustment does God want you to keep in mind to help you with acceptance in your trials?

    1) Trials will happen!

    2) Trials will meet us in the natural pathways of our lives!

    3) Trials will come in many sizes, shapes, shades, and degrees!

    4) Trials will test our faith!

6. **"One Degree Off Course":** What are two thoughts, attitudes, actions, or influences that cause you to get off God's course for you? What are the consequences of those? What can you do this week to get back on God's course for you?

Chapter 3

WHEN WILL I EVER USE THIS IN REAL LIFE?

Understand Our Trials Accomplish God's Purpose

James 1:3-4

"The Greeks had a race in their Olympic games that was unique. The winner was not the runner who finished first. It was the runner who finished with his torch still lit. I want to run all the way with the flame of my torch still lit for Him."

-Joseph Stowell, *Fan The Flame*[1]

Mr. Kennedy and the Question

Amanda frantically waved her arm from side to side barely, missing the students seated in the rows beside and in front of her. Amanda was one of the best math students Mr. Kennedy had, and he knew that her question would be a significant one. Perhaps his love for math had inspired her to become a rocket scientist, an accountant, solve world hunger, or could he dare let himself think, a high school math teacher! With anticipation of a life-changing question, Mr. Kennedy said, "Yes, Amanda." Amanda's reply was that often thought and many times voiced question, "When will I ever use this in real life?"

For nearly 40 years, Dave Kennedy has taught math in the public school system in Indiana and as a mathematics instructor at a local university. This was not a new question nor a new attempt to sidetrack him. Mr. Kennedy gives this insight into answering the question, "When will I ever use this in is real life?"

> This question comes up several times a semester and even on occasion several times a day. There are many different ways to answer this question and it is very difficult to persuade students that what we are doing now will affect them years into the future. A student like Amanda who is motivated to learn will often accept the fact that she might need math in the future and learn what she needs to know by trusting what I told her. I have often had students like Amanda who come back to see me or send an email when they get to college to confirm that they really did need many of the concepts they learned.
>
> On the other hand, I have had students that will ignore almost every example I give which shows them the need for math in order to be well-rounded and prepared for what

might face them in their future. These students also have contacted me after leaving school and have expressed regret for not doing the work when they had the opportunity. They may have decided to go on to college, work in the building trades, or try to start their own business. Now they realize math is something they needed to know.

It is very hard for high school students, as well as those of us in the school of life, to do things and work hard when we can't see the immediate value and uses for our efforts. I often ask students what they will be doing in 10 to 20 years. Most students admit they have no idea. At this point, I try to convince them that as they learn and gain knowledge now, it will lead to more options and opportunities in the future.[2]

How many times does God use the test of trials in our lives to bring about His desired life change, yet we get side-tracked by asking questions like: "When will I ever use this in real life?" What does this have to do with my life?" "Why is God allowing this trial in my life?" When we say this, we have neither fully grasped nor fully accepted God's purpose in trials. Whether we recognize it or not, the tests of trials, more than academics, prepare us for life both now and in eternity. God is not bringing or allowing the tests

> ### When will I ever use this is real life?
>
> *This question can be used to deflect learning, but if we drill deeper, behind this question lies a desire to know purpose and significance.*

of trials in our life as "busy work" to fill up time on earth, nor is he dreaming up new ways to make our life miserable. Each and every trial we experience has real life implications. When we can embrace our trials, they become avenues to God's purpose. We can pass the

test of trials as we understand our trials accomplish God's purpose:
1) to demonstrate our faith is genuine; 2) to develop our maturity in
Christ.

God's Purpose in Trials is to Demonstrate Our Faith is Genuine.   James 1:3

Because you know that the testing of your faith develops perseverance.

James 1:3

"Why?" is the pressing question that squeezes our minds,
our emotions, and even our wills into looking for some reason during
our times of challenges. Often, the answer that comes back to us
is: a loud silence. When we don't receive an answer, it may make us
feel God doesn't care, is trying to punish us, or doesn't exist. When
we do receive an answer, it may not be the one we are hoping for,
and so we keep asking for a different one.   Whether we can see it
or not, whether we accept it or not, God is continually at work in
each of our lives and perhaps never more so than during the test of
trials. As we excavate the mines of purpose and reasons for trials, it
is critical that we keep in mind God's perspective. Because we are
digging deep, if we are off by one degree, we can miss the purpose
God has for the trials of our lives.

As we begin to mine the depths of purpose in trials, we need
God to shine light on the direction we are to dig for we have reached
the very core of what James is saying, the mother lode, so to speak.
The first purpose uncovered is that **trials will prove our faith is
genuine** (James 1:3a).

On our quest, James illuminates the fact that God is intentional and not haphazard with our lives. James begins verse three with the word "because" and uses it to make a statement of purpose. He continues to shine light on the fact that we know God is testing our faith. This may seem like a no-brainer, but the word "know" is a significant gem we have unearthed. The word used for "know" is the Greek word *ginosko*. "*Ginosko* expresses knowledge existent through constant experience."[3] The meaning is "to know by experience or to allow someone or something to experience it with us." It is not that we mentally know that God brings trials with purpose, but that we know God as He participates with us in our trials and that we experience His purpose in our trials. There is a difference between only knowing God intellectually and knowing Him as an active participant in our trials. A comparison between Michael Jordan and my wife will polish this treasured gem and will release the magnificent brilliance of *ginosko* - to know.

One of my favorite basketball players is Michael Jordan. I can tell you a few facts I know about him: he grew up in North Carolina; he was cut from a high school team; he is 6'6"; he won six NBA titles with the Chicago Bulls; tried his hand at baseball in the Chicago White Sox organization; at this time, he is 90% owner of the Charlotte Hornets; he is in his second marriage; he is a billionaire. Michael Jordan and I have never done anything together in life. I have not experienced a basketball game as a spectator in which he played. In comparison, I can also tell you a few things I know about my wife. She grew up on a hog farm in rural Nebraska, where I had an opportunity to visit on several occasions. She is one of eight children, and I have met all of her siblings. She played volleyball and basketball in college where I was able to watch her play in person. My wife and I have experienced

> # KNOW
>
> *Know [ginosko] has the idea of: "to know by experience or to allow someone or to experience something together with us."*

a lot of life together. We have laughed, cried, and been angry with each other. A few places we have enjoyed together are Hawaii, St. Thomas, and Mexico. We have three children and have ministered together for nearly 30 years. I know facts about Michael Jordan, but I know my wife because we have done life together. These two usages of the word "know" are worlds apart. We can know all about the test of trials and we can know all the attributes of God, but until we experience them and allow God to walk through trials with us, we don't really know God or understand the purpose of trials.

As we dig deeper into James' writing, we discover an important gem in the word "testing": *"because you know that the **testing** of your faith…"* (James 1:3a). We must pause, take time, dust it off, and attentively examine this precious jewel we have unearthed. Upon close examination, we note that the word for testing [*dokimion*] used here means: "approved after testing, tested and approved, the genuine part."[4] This word is used to denote the process of refining silver or gold. One commentator provides his cleaning brush to help clear away the dirt in order to take in the sparkling beauty of our gem. "The 'testing of faith' here, then, is not intended to determine whether a person has faith or not; it is intended to purify faith that already exists."[5] In the midst of our trials, God is using them to prove the strength and authenticity of our faith.

The 1972 Miami Dolphins were 17-0 and boast the record of the only NFL football team to go undefeated for the entire regular season, playoffs, and Super Bowl. That year, my brother-in-law waited patiently outside their training facility and gathered autographs from the players on a football. He graciously gave that football to me as a Christmas gift. Even though I know the autographs are genuine, if I were to sell the football, I would have to ask someone who has the ability and authority to prove the

---

Peter's letter reveals the same gems that we find in James' letter.

"In all this you greatly rejoice [**Perspective-joy**], though now for a little while you may have had to suffer grief in all kinds [**word for polka dots**] of trials [**trials-*peirasmos***]. These have come so that [**Purpose**] the proven genuineness [**word for testing-*dokimion***] of your faith [**making the faith our own**]—of greater worth than gold, which perishes even though refined [**word for testing**] by [**this testing happens**] fire—may result in praise, glory and honor when Jesus Christ is revealed [**God's Promise - see James 1:12**]"

1 Peter 1:6-7

---

signatures are real. He would validate the autographs as genuine and give me a certificate of authenticity. Similarly, God is intentionally bringing and allowing trials in our lives in order to place on us the seal of authentic faith. We receive "a certificate of authenticity" that our faith is proved genuine in a particular area of our lives.

The old adage is true, "Don't pray for patience because God will give you trials." God is continually using life's events to make our faith more and more real and genuine. As we give the gem a thorough cleaning, notice this is not just any faith, it is **your** faith. Faith becomes our own as exhibited by the words "your faith". God is active in our lives to make the faith we say we profess into faith that we live out in our daily lives. Just as parents want their children's faith to become their own and not just the parents', God, our heavenly Father, uses the testing of our faith to show us where our faith is our own and where it is not. Trials may come again and again in a particular area of our lives to demonstrate we don't fully trust God with that area. The heat of the trial is used to purify our faith.

This proving of our faith produces endurance or perseverance; *"the testing of your faith, develops perseverance"* (James 1:3b). The discovery of the word perseverance is another gem we want to give meticulous attention. It means to remain under or stand fast. The word focuses primarily on enduring trying circumstances. "The picture is of a person successfully carrying a heavy load for a long time."[6]

In his classical commentary on the book of James, Spiros Zodhiates' light on the gem of endurance or perseverance (*hupomonee*) creates a fascinating luster:

> But the word *hupomenoo*, 'to be patient,' also means 'to remain alive, to be permanent.' Back of it there is the thought of the constancy and perseverance of pressure from the outside world. But the one who has *hupomonee* or 'patience' stays alive permanently under this pressure, no matter how long it lasts.[7]

In the movie *Facing the Giants*, head football coach Grant Taylor works to change the attitudes and culture of his football team. They need to be challenged to do their best and not give up before the game even starts. The team has just concluded the death crawl drill, a drill where a player walks on all fours for ten yards with another player on his back. Coach Taylor calls out one of his players. Brock Hill has incredible leadership abilities, yet doubts his own resolve. Coach asks Brock if he will give his best and Brock agrees. Coach now blindfolds him and has another player climb on his back. The blindfold is to test Brock and see if he will do his best, and not quit when he thinks he's gone far enough. Coach Taylor tells Brock that he believes he can execute the death crawl from the end zone to the 50-yard line, halfway across the football field. Brock starts strong but soon begins to hurt and complain. Coach is yelling for Brock not to give up until he has given his absolute best and all he has. Brock's teammates have been lounging on the grass watching with laughter. Now they rise to their feet with a fresh interest. Coach Taylor is on the ground in front of Brock urging him to endure the pain and agony and focus on giving his very best. Finally, Coach tells him to stop. Brock falls flat on his face and stomach. Coach laying on the ground in front of him asks if he has given all he had. The exhausted player says "yes," and Taylor whispers, "Then take off the blindfold." Instead of fifty yards, Brock Hill had carried his teammate one hundred yards, from end zone to end zone. He had endured the weight of his teammate, undergone burning pain, and proved the genuineness of his heart. Brock needed to be put to the test in order to demonstrate to himself and his teammates he would be a team leader by giving his all. Jesus is doing the same to us. He puts a trial on our backs and asks us to give our all to Him. Jesus asks us trust Him to enable us to carry a heavy load for a long time and to go further than we thought we could. Jesus asks us to listen to the urging of His voice and endure the test until He lets us know we've reached the end zone at the other end of the trial.

By using this same word for perseverance to describe Job's experience, James' own words best clean away the debris from this gem. James gives us this nugget in chapter 5 verse 11, *"As you know, we consider blessed those who have **persevered**. You have heard of Job's **perseverance** and have seen what the Lord finally brought about. The Lord is full of compassion and mercy."* Job experienced unimaginable trials as he lost his livestock (which represented his wealth), his children, and even his health (see Job 1-2). Our friend Job, hung in there under the trials and testing until

---

"I do not pray for a lighter load, but for a stronger back."

-Phillips Brooks, Preacher[8]
Wrote the lyrics to "O Little Town of Bethlehem" in 1868

he came to know or allow God to participate in his life in a way he never would have without the trials (see Job 38-42:6). Eventually, God restored to him his livestock, family, and health (see Job 42:7-17).

Before Job's troubles began, this was God's description of Job: *"He (Job) is the finest man in all the earth. He is blameless—a man of complete integrity. He fears God and stays away from evil"* (Job 1:8b NLT). We must not miss the point in the account of Job. The point was not only did he received back all he lost, but also the fact that as a godly man Job wrestled and struggled with the trial he went through. Finally, he allowed God to participate in his trials. He came to know God more intimately. He hung in there under the trial, and his faith in these areas became increasingly his own. Too many times we buy into the thinking that because I'm a Christian, I live a fairly godly life, and I do more good deeds than my friends, then I am exempt from problems and trials. But nothing could be further from the truth.

> *"Sometimes you face difficulties not because you're doing something wrong, but because you're doing something right."[9]*

There is something lurking in the shadows of our minds. We may feel guilty for even allowing it to take up space in our thoughts, but we know it is a valid question. At times it creeps to the forefront of our minds demanding our attention. If our faith cannot withstand tough questions, what good is it? If as a believer in the Lord Jesus Christ, we will have more trouble and trials than a non-believer, why live for Jesus? There is no simple to this nagging question. It cannot be brushed off with a Christian cliché or even comprehended this side of heaven. The answer is intertwined with the trial or challenge itself. Because Jesus is committed and has promised to continually be active in our lives until His work is fully complete, He will do whatever it takes to accomplish it (Philippians 1:6). Jesus allows or brings these trials into our lives to validate and cultivate our faith as we faithfully persist in our movement towards Him. Oddly, life's trials are a display of Jesus' love for us and His intricate involvement in our lives. Jesus' desire is for an unbeliever to come to saving faith in Him, to move from darkness to light. Then He can turn up the heat of shaping that individual into the person He can use to tell His story of grace. Not a one size fits all answer but thoughts to guide us in the challenges of life. As we address the question, "If I will experience more difficulties in life as a believer in Christ, why follow Jesus Christ?", the Apostle Paul's words are a motivation for us to keep on keeping on, *"Let us not lose heart in doing good, for in due time we will reap if we do not grow weary"* (Galatians 6:9 NASB).

Right now, as you are trudging through the deep and dark mines of trials, feeling lost in the darkness of not knowing the direction to take, and questioning God's reasons, keep placing one foot in front of the other. Continue to remain under the trial until it accomplishes its purpose and you demonstrate your faith is authentic.

"Trials are the crucible in which perseverance is forged."

-Unknown

Several years ago, I was at a youth ministry seminar. The speaker shared with us about a meeting with parents of teens. The question posed was, "If you are living for God, what will that look like?" Answers were along the lines of: "My child would never get cut from a sports team." "My child will not have a serious illness." "My child won't have serious emotional issues or a major break up." "I would never lose my job or have any financial setbacks." Those answers might sound a bit ridiculous as we read them, but how many times have we bought into the lie: I'm living for God or doing good things, then He won't let any "serious" problems into my life. If I experience trials, then God is no longer good, or He is not strong enough to keep bad things away. Maybe, we need to let God, be God!

God's Purpose in Trials is to Develop Our Faith into the Maturity of Christ. James 1:4

Perseverance must finish its work so
that you may be mature and complete,
not lacking anything.

James 1:4

Sometimes, the question of "why" must be replaced with the question of "what." James moves from why God brings trials to what God is doing in trials. Why the testing of our faith? Because God wants us to demonstrate our faith is real. What is God doing in the testing of our faith? He is developing our spiritual maturity to be more and more like Jesus Christ. Honestly, the lantern of "why" does not always give us enough light to see its answer, but the lantern of "what" does gives clarity to see what God is doing.

In verse four, James uses the Greek word *telios* which means complete or mature.[10] He uses it two times; each time the context suggests a different understanding of the word. *"Perseverance must finish (telios) its work."* In John 19:30, the verb form of this word (*teleo*) is used by our Lord Jesus Christ when He said, "It is finished." Just as Jesus accomplished everything the Father prescribed for Him to do, so we too must allow this work of perseverance under trials to accomplish God purposes in our lives.

James emphasizes the reason for our persevering under trials by saying, *"so that you may be mature (telios) and complete not lacking anything."* The reason for the trials in our lives is that we will be "mature and complete." This time James uses the word *telios* to mean "mature." Not only does it mean to accomplish or finish its work but it carries the idea of bringing to maturity. James also adds another word "complete," meaning "complete in all its parts, entire."[11] We may not know this side of heaven "why" we experience certain trials, but we can rest in "what" God is doing. God is using each one of our trials to accomplish spiritual maturity and completeness in every aspect, area, and character trait within us. This gives us further reason to have God's perspective of joy and acceptance in our test of trials. This gives us confidence to surrender ourselves to the Master and Controller, Jesus Christ.

Even when we don't know the why of our trials, which we desperately want to know, it is important to have confidence to trust ourselves to the Master and Controller, Jesus Christ. James has given us a marvelous connection to Job and how his life reflects light on this gem of perseverance. It is my opinion that Job never knew this side of heaven the why behind his trial. We are given information to which Job is not privy. It began with a discussion between God and Satan found in Job 2:3-6, information Job was not given. When Job arrived in heaven, God must have said, "My servant Job, sit down here a minute. I have something to tell you."

> As you know, we count as blessed those who have persevered. You have heard of Job's perseverance and have seen what the Lord finally brought about. The Lord is full of compassion and mercy.
>
> James 5:11

Job did come to understand what God was doing during his time of trial. It taught this "blameless man" to know God more intimately in the midst of having everything stripped away. Job was put in a place where he learned that God was all he needed. As evidenced by Job 38-42, Job realized God had made him more spiritually mature and complete.

The same is true for us in our trials and challenges. We may not know exactly what God is doing but we can be sure He is accomplishing His work in us. As we place this gem of perseverance under the magnifying glass again, we notice one more area radiating from this gem. God is accomplishing His work, so that we will not be found lacking in anything. The NET Bible puts it in clear, simple terms: *"not deficient in anything."*

Discovered in this mine is a vein worth our brief exploration. In the depths of the mine we call trials, there is enough light to see

God obviously has purpose, but even so this mine is not easily navigated. Admittedly, at times the light we have in the mine will be dim. The darkness of fears, questions about and to God, and the personal struggles that accompany our attempts to pass the tests of trials will close in around us as though we only have a flickering candle to feebly light our way.

Here we can turn to the great promise found in Romans 8:28 to bring needed light: *"And we know that in all things God works for the good of those who love Him, who have been called according to His purpose."* However, a word of caution is in order so that the powerful light of this verse is not turned on too quickly or strongly in the darkness of challenges that we blind individuals, causing more harm than encouragement. I love to ask: what does Romans 8:29 say? Most of us know Romans 8:28 but don't know or stumble through Romans 8:29. After we read that in *"all things God works for the good of those who love Him,"* the next verse tells us the reason. *"For those God foreknew He also predestined **to be conformed to the likeness of His Son**, that He might be the firstborn among many brothers"* (Romans 8:29). Don't stumble over the big theological words. Paul and James are expanding each other's thoughts. God's purpose in everything, including trials, is that we would reflect Jesus Christ. We must remember a trial is a test, and a test is the battleground of our wills and controls. The trials that come our way are not going to be easy, even when we know God has a purpose and is at work during our trials. They become even harder, when we struggle with God's purpose and continually ask, "When will I ever use this in real life?"

In graduate school, I had a professor who has deeply and forever impacted my understanding of God and His Word. I always say, "He will forget more about God than I will ever know." One winter, the professor's eldest son was driving when he hit a patch of black ice. The car wreck inflicted the professor with injuries, leaving him in a coma. His younger son was not as fortunate, as the auto accident took his life. By the time our professor came out of the coma, his son's funeral and burial was conducted. A few years later in class, he opened his heart and expressed his struggle with Romans 8:28. He was grappling with what he knew about God from His Word and his own experience. Candidly, he shared the fact that he could not see any good resulting from his son's death. To his knowledge, no one came to know the Lord as Savior, nor did anyone make a significant change in their walk with Christ. At the time, there was not anything tangible he could sense. This professor, who has given his life to the study of the Word of God, did not doubt God or His Word, but he did let us see a man who walked closely with God, knew Him deeply, and still wrestled with the trials in his life.

Dear friends, don't be surprised at the fiery trials you are going through, as if something strange were happening to you. Instead, be very glad—for these trials make you partners with Christ in his suffering, so that you will have the wonderful joy of seeing his glory when it is revealed to all the world.

1 Peter 4:12-13, (NLT)

Interestingly, my wife had a very different perspective. She thought God had used this "accident" for His good and to work in many individual's lives. She was a student at the college during the professor's wreck and recovery. The college began an annual fundraising basketball tournament named after the professor. Initially it helped with his expenses, and then in subsequent years the tournament raised money for someone in need. My wife reflected on how this tragedy brought the school's students together in prayer, community, and service. Surely God was at work during this time. Some could sense what God was doing, and some struggled with it. That is not an indictment on godliness, spirituality, or the lack of it. It is the reality of passing the test of trials. It is a challenge for us to be sensitive to how each of us can be at different places in the trials we are facing in our pathways of life.

As we travel the treacherous terrain of trials, let us seek to understand one another the struggles, the doubts, and the victories. We must be discerning to shine the right amount of light for each person's next step toward becoming more like Jesus Christ.

The Greatest Last Place Finish in Olympic History

The race of life set out before us reveals whether our character is Christ-like. It also gives us an opportunity to develop our character to become like His. Let's take a look at a man who ran a race he had run many times before, but on this occasion it clearly revealed and developed his character.

On a sweltering Sunday in October of 1968, in the high altitude of Mexico City, the athletes were preparing to run their race. At a little past 3 pm local time, the next scheduled event for these Olympic Games was the marathon. It was a race of 26 miles and 385 yards (42.195 kilometers) that would require the participants to use every bit of grit and fortitude they could muster. In fact, only 57 of the 75 competitors who began this particular Olympic marathon would finish the race. Intrigue surrounded this event, as two world class runners would contend with each other and the rest of the pack for the chance at the gold medal. The two runners were John Stephen Akhwari of Tanzania and Mamo Wolde of Ethiopia. In their previous race, Akhwari had defeated Wolde, so the stage was set for an incredible race and an unforgettable finish. Akhwari own words describe what happened as the race unfolded:

> When I arrived in Mexico City for the 1968 Olympics, I was afraid of nothing. But I wasn't prepared for the altitude; my country had sent me to train at sea level in Dar es Salaam [Tanzania]. I was leading until the 30K mark, when I suddenly felt dizzy. I fell and blacked out. I have no idea how much time I lost. When I woke up, the medical team was treating me. They asked me to get in an ambulance, but I refused—I just started running and walking. I was in a lot of pain and was bleeding; I had injured both knees and torn several tendons. But I did not care; my main mission was to finish.[12]

The first runner finished the race with a time of 2:20:26. It was Mamo Wolde of Ethiopia who would stand on the podium as 1968 Olympic marathon gold medal winner. The other runners finished, and now the clock showed almost 7pm on that Mexico City night. The sky started to darken and the spectators had been filtering out of the stadium. It was over an hour after Wolde finished his race when police sirens and flashing lights became a magnet drawing the attention of any individuals still in the stadium. What appeared next from the stadium's gate was a lone runner, proudly wearing the colors of Tanzania. Leg bandaged and bleeding, limping and exhausted, the runner pulled together every ounce of his perseverance he could muster and pushed himself to finish the race with a time of 3:35:27. When asked why he did not stop running, John Stephen Akhwari said, "My country did not send me 5,000 miles just to start the race; they sent me to finish the race."

John Stephen Akhwari gave us a physical example to follow as we hear the challenge to run the spiritual race, *"let us run with endurance the race God has set before us."* **We do this by keeping our eyes on Jesus!**

Without purpose, it is difficult for us to "keep on keeping on." Now that we are

> Therefore, since we are surrounded by such a huge crowd of witnesses to the life of faith, let us strip off every weight that slows us down, especially the sin that so easily trips us up. And let us run with **endurance** the race God has set before us. We do this by keeping our eyes on Jesus, the champion who initiates and perfects our faith. Because of the joy awaiting him, he **endured** the cross, disregarding its shame. Now he is seated in the place of honor beside God's throne.
>
> Hebrews 12:1-2 (NLT)

equipped with God's purpose in our trials, we can have the tenacity to put one foot in front of the other to run with endurance. In the marathon of the trials of life, purpose gives us hope: nevertheless, we still come to God to plead for His guidance and wisdom. God delights in our prayers during trials, and next James gives us three ways to allow our trials to teach us God's prayer.

WHEN WILL I EVER USE THIS IN REAL LIFE?

Understand our trials accomplish God's Purpose; James 1:3-4

- Think About It & Talk About It -

1. Describe a time you said, "When will I ever use this in real life?" What was your real reason for asking the question?

2. Our definition of trials is: **"A trial is a test God uses to prove the genuineness of our faith and to develop our maturity in Jesus Christ."** From this definition, what do you want to remember during your trials? What questions do you have regarding trials?

3. **"A trial is a test God uses to prove the genuineness of our faith."** How does God use trials to authenticate the genuineness of our faith? How does God use trials to reveal our faith?

4. ***"A trial is a test God uses to develop our maturity in Jesus Christ."*** How does God use trials to develop our maturity in Jesus Christ? How does God use trials to develop our faith?

5. What do you learn from the story of John Stephen Akhwari? How does Akhwari's story illustrate the role perseverance in trials? Explain.

Chapter 4

ISN'T
THE LEARNING CENTER
FOR DUMMIES?

Allow Our Trials To Teach Us
God's Prayer

James 1:5-8

"Contrary to popular opinion,
prayer is the most tangible and practical thing
we can do in the face of a crisis."

-Gary Mayes, *Now What!*[1]

THE LEARNING CENTER

The summer before my middle son went to the University of Central Missouri, we attended an orientation. My attention perked up when they discussed the Learning Center on campus. During the presentation it was stressed that many of the students who went to the learning center did not go because they were struggling academically. They utilized the services because they wanted to turn their "B" papers into "A" papers. Those comments brought me back to my days as a college Instructor, where the same was true at that school. The stigma that "the Learning Center is for dummies" dissipates when we realize it is really the smart students who choose to use the services. The Learning Center at institutions is there to aid students in their studies whether they are struggling to pass or working to get a better grade.

Maybe our pride, the desire to be "self-made," the fear of revealing a weakness, or a myriad of other

THE TEST PRAYER

Now I lay me down to study;
I pray the Lord I won't go nutty.
If I should fail to learn this junk;
I pray to the Lord I will not flunk.
But if I do, don't pity me at all,
Just lay my bones down in study hall.
Tell my instructor I did my best,
Then pile my books upon my chest.
Now I lay me down to rest,
And pray I'll pass tomorrow's test.
If I should die before I wake,
That's one less test I'll have to take

-Unknown

reasons, it can be difficult for us to reach out to receive help in certain areas of our lives. Individuals have told me, "I learn best on my own and from my own experience." But Proverbs instructs us that it is the wise person who will heed these words: *"Incline your ear, and hear the words of the wise, and apply your heart to my knowledge, for it will be pleasant if you keep them within you, if all of them are ready on your lips"* (Proverbs 22:17-18 ESV). *"Do you see a person wise in their own eyes? There is more hope for a fool than for them"* (Proverbs 26:12). We are instructed to listen and learn from others, not just muddle our way through life's trials, trying to learn on our own.

Here is where prayer comes in to overcome life's challenges. Prayer is not merely for those who need a crutch to lean on in difficulties. Instead we are commanded to pray and ask for wisdom during our trials. Whether we are failing the tests of trials or just want to improve, prayer is one of the key components of aligning ourselves with God's perspective and accomplishing God's purpose during our seasons of trials. It is comparable to a college Learning Center.

In recent months, the other side of the coin has aroused my interest as well. I am around many individuals who claim to be Christians but keep God at arm's length in everyday matters. Others are unbelievers, yet when tragedy strikes they state "their thoughts and prayers" are with the one going through the affliction or trial.

> *"Pray the hardest when it is hardest to pray."*

There are many who turn to God in the times of trials seeking some divine intervention. They come to the learning center of prayer because they need help. This can be seen in the public school system. Though public prayer has been outlawed by the government, I can guarantee you that before tests, prayers are being offered by the bright and the not so bright, the believer and the non-believer.

The great and comforting news is that God has not outlawed prayer for His tests, but in fact He encourages and commands us to pray and to seek Him for wisdom in each of our challenges. James gives us three ways to allow trials to teach us how God wants us to pray in times of trials. The gospels record what is typically referred to as the "The Lord's Prayer." It has been suggested that it really is "The Apostles' Prayer" because Jesus is teaching them how to prayer. Comparably James gives us principles on how to pray in the throes of trials, and we shall call it "God's Prayer." Lest we miscommunicate, it is not God praying for us but God who gives us instructions for our prayer to Him. God's prayer teaches us: 1) to look at our trials from God's viewpoint; 2) to commit our trials to God's character; 3) to entrust our trials to God wholeheartedly.

God's Prayer Teaches Us to Look at Our Trials from God's Viewpoint   James 1:5a

If any of you lacks wisdom, he should ask God,

James 1:5a

The famous English preacher from the late 1800's Charles H. Spurgeon, once stated, "Prayer moves the arm that moves the world...You can be omnipotent [all-powerful] if you know how to pray, omnipotent in all things that glorify God...Prayer is the slender nerve that moves the muscles of Omnipotence."[2] Having just discussed God's perspective and God's purpose in trials, James moves to that tiny nerve in our spiritual being that can move an all-powerful God: prayer. Notice the three principles we have already examined tie into James' next principle for passing tests by allowing trials to teach us the principles of God's prayer. **God's perspective** and **God's purpose** in trials are large muscles, that move by **God's power** through the tiny nerve of **Prayer**.

In verse five, James makes some interesting connections. *"But if anyone is deficient in wisdom, he should ask God"* (NET). Notice the contrast: *"But if."* In verse four James tells us that one of God's purposes in our trials is that we will be mature and complete, not lacking in anything. If we cannot see our trial from God's perspective, ask Him to show us. God's desire is that we will not be deficient but complete. Instead of an afterthought, God instructs prayer as our first thought when we encounter the challenges of life.

The words, *"But if we lack wisdom,"* connect us back to verse two where James tells us we need to see trials from God's perspective and respond accordingly. This is wisdom. Here in verse five, God reveals His heart for us. He wants us to have this wisdom which is His perspective of joy and acceptance in the middle of our test of trials. So, we are commanded to ask for wisdom.

Plainly, if we want wisdom or are deficient in wisdom during trials, we need to ask God. This can be a lot like being in the Learning Center. We may need to pray to ask God for even a desire to see life from His perspective. We may need to pray to take the next step in our walk with Jesus. We may know what God's perspective is, but we need to pray to be able to respond according to that worldview. We may need to pray because we are clueless about what God is doing in our lives and what lens He wants us to use in order to see our circumstances shaded the way He does. Paul speaks about not knowing how to pray in times of suffering but his words of comfort to the suffering apply to those who are experiencing trials, also. Right now, as your trial stares menacingly into your eyes and stands seemly unconquerable in your path, let these words be a comfort to your mind and minister to your heart, *"In the same way, the Spirit helps us in our weakness. We do not know what we ought to pray for, but the Spirit himself intercedes for us through wordless groans. And he who searches our hearts knows the mind of the Spirit, because the Spirit intercedes for God's people in accordance with the will of God"* (Romans 8:26-27).

The prayer that God wants from us may be likened to a parade. At a parade, we stand on the side of the street or at a corner. As we watch the parade, we see what is in front of us. We can also see what has just passed and can remember what has gone by earlier. But we can only catch a glimpse of what is coming. We might crane our necks or sit on the shoulders of someone else, but we can only see so far. However, if we were to get in a helicopter and fly above the parade, we would be able to see the beginning, the end of the parade, and everything between. We could see the band from our local high school is first, followed by some clowns on unicycles. In the middle is a group of cheerleaders riding in convertibles throwing out candy. At the end of the parade, we see the mayor on a motorcycle followed by the local fire department with their big hook and ladder truck. The parade is like our lives, and we are standing on the side of the street. We can remember what has happened, see what is in front of us, but only wonder about what is to come. That is our natural perspective, but God wants us to pray that we might ride in the helicopter. Being in the helicopter and seeing the whole parade is to see our whole life from God's perspective, which is wisdom. We can see everything from His viewpoint. The prayer God prescribes leads us to this: "Whether you can see God at work or not has nothing to do with whether He is at work or not!"[3]

This wisdom is available for anyone who desires, it and we are commanded to ask God for it. In times of trials, we are to be driven to God, not anyone or anything else. Each of us has our tendencies during times of trouble. We try to be self-sustaining by looking inside ourselves for answers. We ask others, seeking to gain advice and insight. We may try to escape through a substance, or by becoming consumed with interests, jobs, or the distractions of life. Not only are we commanded to ask God, but also the word "ask" itself directs us to take our requests to Him. The word "ask" carries the idea of someone in a lesser position (us) making a request to someone in a greater position (God). What tremendous encouragement to come to God in prayer is nestled in the book of Hebrews, *"Let us then with confidence draw near to the throne of grace, that we may receive mercy and find grace to help in time of need"* (Hebrews 4:16 ESV).

This asking is to be done with a sense of urgency, begging, or desiring. When we encounter trials of all kinds, shapes, colors, and from different directions, God wants us to come to Him, desperately seeking Him. It is during times of trial that we seek and find God, and that's what God wants. Give thought to this observation: "And if a believer who is being tested is not driven to the Lord and does not develop a deeper prayer life, the Lord is likely to keep the test active and even intensify it until His child comes to the throne of grace - until he makes his 'ear attentive to wisdom,' and inclines his 'heart to understanding' (Prov. 2:2.)."[4]

God's Prayer Teaches Us to Commit Our Trials to God's Character   James 1:5b

Who gives generously to all without finding fault,
and it will be given to him.

James 1:5b

Going to the pool with little children can provide great entertainment and incredible exhaustion. My boys loved to jump off the side of the pool into my arms over and over and over, until I could no longer lift them. The boys would jump with no fear, even though the water was be over their heads and their swimming skills shaky. They trusted me to catch them every time, even when I wasn't looking or wasn't ready. They knew that Dad had the ability to keep them from the potential dangers of the water, and they threw themselves at me with huge smiles and reckless abandon. At the same pool, there were kids that would allow their fears of the water and uncertainties in the one catching them to keep them from jumping. If they did jump, they did so with hesitation. In the same way, we jump to the arms of our Savior in potential danger, because we know and trust His character. Or we allow fears to block our reliance on the character of our trustworthy Lord Jesus Christ.

Amazingly, we will jump off the side of the pool and trust Jesus to catch us in one trial. Then in very next trial, fear, doubt, questions, grumbling, and complaining will keep us from jumping.

From cover to cover in the Word of God, we find people doing the same thing. When the Bible speaks of God's power, it often refers to one of three unparalleled events: the creation of the world, the resurrection of Jesus Christ, and God's parting the waters of the Red Sea.

> Now these things occurred as examples to keep us from setting our hearts on evil things as they did.
>
> 1 Corinthians 10:6

The very Israelites who crossed the Red Sea went between the walls of water and saw their enemies the Egyptians drown. Not one of their sandals got stuck in the mud because the ground was dry. Shortly thereafter these same Israelites allowed doubts, fears, and questions to invade their ranks. This infiltration grew to the point that they decided God would not be able to handle their next trial. They complained about the food God provided, because it was not what they wanted. They became inpatient and worshipped a golden calf, because God seemed too slow and distant for their liking. They doubted their powerful God when He promised victory in taking the land, because their fear of man was greater than their fear of God. They witnessed firsthand one of the most recognizable and inconceivable miracles in all of the Word of God, yet these same Israelites did not know their God or trust their Red Sea-parting-God with the very next test.

Unfortunately, we are just like the Israelites. God can "part the Red Sea" in our lives, and then at the very next challenge we complain, become inpatient, focus our attention on something else, and doubt the Almighty. We, too, quickly forget who God is and what He has done. The Bible is a book about God, and we must constantly search the Scriptures to understand and focus on the character and nature of our God, especially during the testing of trials, because we are so easily distracted. This is what James is instructing us. The only way we will look at our trials from God's perspective is to know our God and how He sees them. Because we are finite and God is infinite, we are urged to plea for wisdom. James next step for us is to commit our trials to the character of God. We cannot ignore Peter's words, *"But grow in the grace and knowledge of our Lord and Savior Jesus Christ"* (2 Peter 3:18a). We also note a marvelous connection between wisdom and the knowledge of God in Proverbs 9:10, *"The fear of the Lord is the beginning of wisdom, and knowledge of the Holy One is understanding."* Pray to be awestruck by Jesus Christ, this is the beginning of wisdom and seeing life from the helicopter. Continue to grow in the knowledge of our Lord and Savior Jesus Christ; this brings understanding. James continues to guide us to travel through life with a greater and greater understanding of the character of God. Before we embark on this journey with James to explore the vastness of Our Savior Jesus Christ: Stop reading! That's right; take a moment to ask the Holy Spirit to expand your grasp of the greatness of our God. As James zeroes in on five character traits of the Holy One to stimulate us to commit our trials to Him in prayer, remember the Holy Spirit is ultimately our Teacher.

First, God is a giving God. James simply states, *"God who gives."* Since it is difficult to have wisdom in trials, let us ask for wisdom from the giving God. God wants us to know what He is doing and to grow in our knowledge of His graciousness. Undoubtedly, the most familiar verse in the entire Bible, John 3:16, *"For God so loved the world that He gave...."* is also the verse about which we can become the most indifferent. In the midst of trials, take time to go over and over this tremendous verse, until the message of God's heart of giving is fresh and alive. Loving is giving!

> ## Giving = Loving
>
> For God so **loved** the world that he **gave** his one and only Son
>
> John 3:16a

Second, God is a generous God. Not only is God a giving God, James paints with vivid colors a picture of that giving by describing it as "generous." This word generous speaks of openheartedness and singleness of heart. God's generous giving means it is unconditional and without bargaining. God gives to us freely.[5] We don't need to pray, "Jesus, if you get me out of this mess or get me through this trial, I will go to church for a month of Sundays!" It is very difficult for those of us walking around in human earth suits to love with no strings attached. To be honest, a lot of our love is tainted by impure motives. Our love is served with a slice of condition. We do this to get something from another. We give to be recognized. We care in order to achieve merit with God. God's love is completely different, and though we know God loves, we must ponder His unfathomable, generous love often. Here, James tells us, it is given unreservedly and freely. "So we praise God for the glorious grace he has poured out on us who belong to his dear Son" (Ephesians 1:6 NLT).

Third, God is an impartial God. This wisdom is given "to all." Gaining insight as we pray in the storms of life is a prayer for each and every one of us. It is a prayer for those of us who just want to pass, and it is a prayer for those of us who want our lives to move from "B's to "A's." The point is that God wants to meet us in each and every testing of our faith, no matter whether we do well on God's tests or if we have to repeatedly take them over. We may battle a sin that wins most of the time. We may wrestle with a decision that is perplexing. We may have walked with God a long time. We may have just passed a huge trial with flying colors. We may not be sure if we even want to follow Jesus. But God is there for us! Romans 2:11 tell us, *"For God does not show favoritism."*

Fourth, God is a gracious God. James connects these two qualities of God's giving together: generous and gracious. Not only does God give freely, but He also gives without finding fault. God is gracious to us. The phrase "without finding fault" means God gives without rebuking, reproving or insulting.[6] Because God wants us to come to Him and ask for wisdom in times of trials, He will never get tired of this request. It brings joy to God's heart when we seek His perspective and His purpose in our trials. He is not going to look down on us or make fun of us because of our struggle with trials, our inability to pass the test, or our continual request for wisdom. Even if that struggle includes impatience, complaints, or doubts about Him, Jesus wants us to come to Him in prayer. I love how my friend John prays. "Lord, we don't demand this of You, but we ask." Use John's words to guide you to honor God with His rightful and revered position, and then to pray boldly to the Lord Jesus Christ. Ponder the powerful account of God's graciousness to us in Romans 5:8, *"But God demonstrates his own love for us in this: While we were still sinners, Christ died for us."*

Fifth, God is a promise-keeping God. James gives us a tremendous and comforting promise, *"and it will be given to him."* It has been said, "That is surely one of the most beautiful and encouraging promises in all of Scripture."[7] God's promise is that His wisdom will be given to us. We need to regularly contemplate God's promises that are rooted in His trustworthy character. Take note, this promise comes with a condition. This condition is not contrary to the fact that God gives without finding fault, nor does it violate God's character of keeping His word to us. This is how God has chosen to construct His promise, which is His prerogative. It is based on two conditions: if we ask God (v.5), and if we believe and do not doubt (v.6). We observe carefully what is promised and what is not promised. God's promise is that we will be able to see the trial the way He sees it and then to live in the path He has marked out for us. It does not say we will fully understand, have the answer to the *why* of the trial, or have the trial taken away, but we will be drawn to the Lord in intimacy and trust. Again, our thoughts gravitate to how much we are like the Israelites because we are impatient, doubt, and complain about God in the midst of our trials. Yet interestingly, tucked away in the pages of an Old Testament book, primarily written to these same doubting Israelites, we are given a precious glimpse of this foundational characteristic of our promise-keeping God. We can build our lives on this foundation. *"God is not a man, so he does not lie. He is not human, so he does not change his mind. Has God ever spoken and failed to act? Has God ever promised and not carried it through?"* (Numbers 23:19 NLT) In our human minds, we may answer yes, but the character and nature of God emphatically answers NO to these questions.

THE RICHES OF GOD'S CHARACTER:

God is a **giving** God.

God is a **generous** God.

God is an **impartial** God.

God is a **gracious** God.

God is a **promise keeping** God.

God's Prayer Teaches Us to Entrust Our Trials to God Wholeheartedly   James 1:6-8

But when he asks, he must believe and not doubt, because he who doubts is like a wave of the sea, blown and tossed by the wind. That man should not think he will receive anything from the Lord; he is a double-minded man, unstable in all he does.

James 1:6-8

Unless we have a proper understanding Who God is, we will not trust Him with our trials. I am reminded of Samuel's interaction with God when the LORD calls his name in 1 Samuel 3:10, "The LORD came and stood there, calling as at the other times, 'Samuel! Samuel!' Then Samuel said, **'Speak, for your servant is listening.'**" So often, our prayer is backward: **"Lord, listen for your servant is speaking."**

Have you ever heard an out-of-tune instrument? Even an instrument slightly out of tune distracts us from the music and can give "the willies" to the trained ear. At one church where I ministered, every six months the piano tuner would come to align the strings of the instrument with the correct musical note. The piano tuner would play a note on the piano, and his ear could tell if it was on the correct pitch or not. He then would use an instrument to adjust the string until it resonated with the pitch it was to sound. Sometimes I would hear the piano tuner playing the same key on the piano over and over several times, adjusting that particular string until it was just where it need to be. God is like the piano tuner. He knows the note we are to sound. The string on the piano is like us. We get out of tune with God. The piano tuning instrument is like the trials in our lives that bring the needed adjustments to put us in harmony with God's song. When we don't align ourselves with the pitch God wants our lives to sound, He continually applies the instrument of trials to bring about His desired outcome.

Going right to the heart of the matter, an old English preacher, Alexander Maclaren,[8] made this convicting statement: ***"The true end of prayer is to get our wills harmonized with His, not to bend His to ours."*** This is a simple, practical, profound, yet terribly difficult statement about entrusting our trials to God wholeheartedly in prayer. God is using the trial we are facing right now to get us on our knees and wrestle with our will and God's will until we are in tune with Him. We may find ourselves praying, "Lord, listen for your servant is speaking!" Allow the Piano Tuner to do His work through the challenges we face.

As we have seen in verse five, God wholeheartedly gives to us. In

"I hear men praying everywhere for more faith, but when I listen to them carefully, and get to the real heart of their prayer, very often it is not more faith at all that they are wanting, but a change from faith to sight. Faith says not, "I see that it is good for me, so God must have sent it," but, "God sent it, and so it must be good for me." Faith, walking in the dark with God only prays Him to clasp its hand more closely."

-Phillips Brooks, American Preacher
December 1835 – January 1893

verses 6-8, James makes a contrast between God's single-heartedness and our double-heartedness. As James progresses into verse six, he uses the word "but" to emphasize a contrast between God and us, *"But when you ask, you must believe and not doubt."* He warns us about doubting God and instructs us to be wholehearted in trusting our trials to Him. Remember God's injunctions for wisdom in our trials: to ask Him and to Him ask in faith. "Here it [faith] means 'confidence in prayer.' It means the petitioner's faith, his belief and trust, that God will heed his prayer and grant it or only in His superior wisdom deny it."[9]

James commands us to pray in faith and then stresses that fact by adding the words "no doubting." Literally, it means "nothing doubting." When we see God for who He is, we will trust Him wholeheartedly. We will not be doubters because our confidence is not contingent on our worthiness but on God's trustworthiness. Earlier James described five character traits of God; now he depicts four traits of a doubter. For the word James uses to paint a doubter, his brush goes to the dismal side of his color palette. His portrait of a doubter is a picture of someone who is fighting with self. It portrays a person who disputes with himself or herself and is divided or wavers. Let's look at how James describes doubters and how we are challenged to be believers.

First, doubters are disputers. As noted, the word for doubt is to be at odds with one's self. "The picture here is not of a wave mounting in height and crashing to shore, but of the swell of the sea, never having the same texture and shape from moment to moment."[10] When we face trials, our biggest battle probably will be with ourselves. Doubting "would designate a battle of the mind, a

114

battle with your own self."[11] Here, the picture is of one arguing or disputing with oneself, going back and forth in what he or she believes should be done, what to believe, and who to trust. Just like the wave at sea, the wind of our thoughts blows us in one direction and then another, and this creates doubt with God. The word "blown" comes from a word meaning bellows and is used primarily for fanning a fire. "James, it seems to me, wants to tell us that unless we come to God with definiteness and singleness of purpose of heart and mind, every little difficulty of life will be like a bellows fanning the fire within us and causing us to be in constant turmoil."[12]

> "With the goodness of God to desire our highest welfare, the wisdom of God to plan it, and the power of God to achieve it, what do we lack?"
>
> -A.W. Tozer

Believers are clingers. They cling to God who is the hope and anchor for their souls, no matter what the winds of doubt try to blow against them. *"So, God has given both his promise and his oath. These two things are unchangeable because it is impossible for God to lie. Therefore, we who have fled to him for refuge can have great confidence as we hold to the hope that lies before us. This hope is a strong and trustworthy anchor for our souls"* (Hebrews 6:18-19 NLT).

Second, doubters are delusional. The doubters, who fight with themselves, should not think they will receive anything from the Lord. When we doubt God or vacillate in our faith, we are only deceiving ourselves into thinking God will answer our prayer.

115

Believers are claimers. They claim the promises of God and pray with confidence according to His will. *"This is the confidence we have in approaching God: that if we ask anything according to his will, he hears us. And if we know that he hears us—whatever we ask—we know that we have what we asked of him"* (1 John 5:14-15).

Third, doubters are divided. Disputing with one's self and delusional thinking leads to division. The word here for doubters means two-souled. They live lives of duplicity, are two-faced, or pulled in different directions. This is the opposite of God's character of wholehearted or single hearted commitment to us. **Believers are committed.** It is in vogue to "keep all our options open," but when it comes to our walk with God we must be wholeheartedly committed to our Savior Jesus Christ. Throughout this chapter, we have seen how often we are like the Israelites. Let us look at the twelve Israelites spies who explored the Promised Land. After spying out the land, ten were doubters. They did not believe God's promise to give them the land, and their doubt divided the nation. Only two were believers. Joshua and Caleb were wholehearted believers committed to stepping out by faith and trusting God during the testing of their faith. We need to have a wholehearted commitment to stand for the Lord when others doubt. *"But because my servant Caleb has a different spirit and follows me wholeheartedly, I will bring him into the land [Promised Land] he went to, and his descendants will inherit it"* (Numbers 14:24).

Fourth, doubters are disastrous. This downward spiral of a doubter has a sad ending. The doubter is unstable in all he does. The three previous descriptions of the doubter culminate in this last, bleak, despondent picture. The word unstable refers to "vacillating in all his activity and conduct." When we are believers and doubt God, we should experience a raging battle within, because we really do want to trust God. If you do not have this battle inside of you, ask yourself, "Am I really a believer?" Or, "Have I become so hardened to the things of the Lord, that it does not bother me to trust other people, things, or myself instead of thrusting the Anchor for my soul – Jesus Christ?" The inward conflict clouds us into thinking our prayers will be answered, even if we don't trust God. When our prayers seem to bounce off the ceiling, the answer to the question "why" is crickets chirping, God seems distant, and we aren't harmonizing our wills with His. We become double-minded and unstable instead of wholehearted in our journey with the Lord. Then our spiritual life is a disaster and we will not pass the test of trials. **Believers are confident**. Jesus makes it clear our confidence and loyalty can only be placed in One. That One is the risen Lord. *"No one can serve two masters. Either you will hate the one and love the other, or you will be devoted to the one and despise the other"* (Matthew 6:24a).

Bread and Milk from Heaven

The time was the 1800's. The place was England. The need was great. The needy were orphans and God chose one of His children to serve the orphans of England. The man was George Müller. Müller would be put through many tests as he sought to feed, clothe, house, and school disadvantaged children. As often happens, this missionary evangelist and coordinator of orphanages labored to make ends meet and provide for the many needs of the orphans. Over the years, God's man, George Müller, would care for over 10,000 orphans, raise millions of dollars, and established 117 schools which offered Christian education to more than 120,000 children. What is most remarkable is that George Müller would never make a request for financial support, nor would he go into debt. He would only make his needs and requests known to God in the secrecy of his prayers.

No one exemplifies what James is saying more than George Müller. As George would pray in times of trial, he would look at the situation from God's viewpoint, he would commit his need to the character of God, and he would trust God wholeheartedly. He was not a doubter but a believer.

One morning the breakfast table was set for the children with plates, bowls, and cups. But they were empty, because there was no food and no money to buy food. As the children were waiting for their breakfast Müller stated, "Children, you know we must be on time for school." He had the 300 children be seated and then prayed, "Dear Father, we thank Thee for what Thou art going to give us to eat." Müller finished his prayer and believed God would provide food for the children, just as He always did. A knock came at the door, and when George opened it, there stood a baker. The baker blurted out, "Mr. Müller, I couldn't sleep last night. Somehow, I felt you didn't have bread for breakfast and the Lord wanted me to send you some. I got

> *"The greater the difficulty to be overcome, the more will it be seen to the glory of God how much can be done by prayer and faith."*
>
> -George Müller[13]

up at 2 am, baked some fresh bread, and here it is." No sooner had George thanked the baker and he left, when there was a second knock at the door. It was the milkman who announced that his milk cart broken down right in front of the orphanage. He wanted to give the children his cans of fresh milk because by the time he emptied his wagon of the weight in order to repair it, the milk would spoil.

He inquired of George if he could use some free milk. George knew in the midst of that trial, he could trust God. God provided bread and milk for 300 children!

George Müller's own words provide us with a tremendous summary of praying as God instructs us in trials and is an inspiration for us during the test of our trials:

> I need not despair because the living God is my partner. I do not have sufficient wisdom to meet these difficulties, but He is able to direct me. I can pour out my heart to God and ask Him to guide and direct me and to supply me with wisdom. Then I have to believe that He will do so. I can go with good courage to my business and expect help from Him in the next difficulty that may come before me.[14]

We tend to run ahead of or lag behind God. We dart right past Him to attack our trials head on with our understanding and strength, not waiting on God in prayer. We set up a tent in the comfort of prayer. When God asks us to move from our place of solace with His understanding and strength, God is waiting on us. Not only does James gives us the recipe for learning to pray God's prayer during the times of trials but prayer also moves us to God's place. As we join James in verses nine through eleven, we uncover some remarkable truths about God's place for every believer in Jesus Christ, especially as we experience the challenges of life.

ISN'T THE LEARNING CENTER FOR DUMMIES?
Allowing Trials to Teach us God's Prayer; James 1:5-8

-Think About It & Talk About It -

1. Identify your tendency: 1) I try to figure out how to handle trials with little or no prayer; 2) I pray and pray, but do little or nothing to deal with the problem. Why do you think you do that?

2. How do our prayers during trials connect with God's perspective and purpose?

3. From the five characteristics of God that James gives us, which one do you need to focus on during your times of trial? Explain.

4. James paints a picture of four kinds of doubters. Which doubter do you most identify with? Why? How can you turn from a doubter to a believer?

5. What comments can you make regarding Alexander Maclaren's statement: **"The true end of prayer is to get our wills harmonized with His, not to bend His to ours."**

6. How does George Müller's life illustrate each of these principles about learning to pray in times of trials?

   a. See God's viewpoint in times of trials

   b. Cling to God's character in the times of trials

   c. Be wholehearted in the times of trials

Chapter 5

DOESN'T MY TEACHER GRADE ON A CURVE?

Let Our Trials Lead Us To God's Place

James 1:9-11

"If I find in myself desires which nothing in this world can satisfy, the only logical explanation is that I was made for another world."

-C.S. Lewis, *Mere Christianity*[1]

Church History with Dr. Bartlett

Dr. Bartlett's picturesque descriptions of events and people, majestic grasp of the English language, and intimate knowledge of history made his classes popular among many college students. His lectures caused history to leap off the pages of the book as though he was a firsthand witness of the people and events. My friend, Steve, was one of his proponents, thus convincing me to take Dr. Bartlett for a two-semester course in Church History.

Dr. Bartlett walked head and shoulders above everyone else in the area of history, and I could never reach his plane. I struggled with taking notes in his class and doing well on his tests. His massive exams, included fill in the blanks and lists, which would literally have to be memorized. I think he was secretly proud that no one ever aced his exams. Dr. Bartlett was also the first instructor I encountered that graded on a curve. This meant that a few people received A's, a few received F's, and most received C's on every test and quiz. In academia, there is a debate representing both the pros and cons of "grading on a curve." Some would say it motivates students because it fosters competition. Others would say that creating competition over a limited number of high grades is more hurtful to motivation than helpful.

Great story but why the discussion of Dr. Bartlett's Church History course and his use of grading on a curve? I'm so glad you asked! And even if you didn't, let me explain the connection to Dr. Bartlett and how we deal with the tests of trials. At times, God can seem a bit like Dr. Bartlett and at the same time very different from him. As God is teaching us the material we need to pass the test of

125

trials, He knows what He is teaching us inside and out. The lessons to learn may be difficult for some of us, yet others may grasp them better than we do. My friend, Steve, did in Church History class and probably in the trials of life. We tend to compare ourselves with others, as I just did. This only leads to pride, "Hey, I'm not so bad!" Or as in my case, discouragement, "Hey, I'm not as good as my friend Steve." The Scripture tells us we are not wise when we compare ourselves to others (2 Corinthians 10:12).

Many of us feel like we are probably in the middle of God's grading curve, not as good as some but definitely better than others. But this is where Dr. Bartlett and God differ. **Our God does not grade on a curve!** The fact is that God holds us against the standard of Jesus Christ, not only for our salvation but for the passing of our tests of trials. God does not throw us into the trial, see how we do, and then pass out grades based on how everyone does. Jesus is the standard for the Christian life and that standard is perfection. Jesus' sinless standard leaves each and every one of us with an "F" when it comes to passing trials. Each of us are on common ground, as James own words tell us, *"For the person who keeps all of the laws except one is as guilty as a person who has broken all of God's laws"* (James 2:10 NLT).

Initially, this may seem disheartening and unfair, but this is the place God wants us to be. This common

> Paul states we are on this common ground because we all have sinned, **"for everyone has sinned; we all fall short of God's glorious standard"** (Romans 3:23 NLT).

ground puts each of us at the foot of the cross to rely completely on the person and work of Jesus Christ. Here is where we find God's place for us in Jesus Christ and overcoming life's challenges. Because the tests of our trials are not graded on a curve but against the standard of Christ, we must let our trials lead us to God's place. God's place is to focus on our position in Christ and not to be distracted by our earthly position. Not only do trials develop us, but they reveal Christlikeness in each of us, as they escort us to God's place. God's place for us in trials is to hold tightly to our position in Christ and loosely to our position on earth.

God's Place for Us in Trials is to Hold Tightly to Our Position in Christ.　　　　James 1:9

Believers in humble circumstances ought
to take pride in their high position.

James 1:9

At some graduation receptions I have attended, there is an intriguing book given to the graduates. It is a book to challenge and inspire the new graduates to blaze their own trail in life, to climb to new heights, and to go to great places. The book is *"Oh, The Places We Go"* written by Dr. Seuss. The book begins, *"Congratulations! Today is your day. You're off to Great Places! You're off and away."* It ends, *"KID, YOU'LL MOVE MOUNTAINS! So...be your name Buxbaum or Bixby or Bray or Mordecai Ali Van*

Allen O'Shea. You're off to Great Places! Today is your Day! Your mountain is waiting. So...get on your way!"[2]

Graduation can be likened to the moment we begin our relationship with Jesus. It is the end of one chapter in a person's life and the beginning of another. At that point, we do not yet know or understand the place God will take us as we embark on this new, grand, glorious, trial and test-filled journey called the Christian life. Just like the cryptic message of that "great theologian," Dr. Seuss, "Oh, the places we go!" On this path through life, a believer may go many places, and as we have discovered he or she will assuredly encounter the test of trials along the way. It is in the maze of these trials that God wants to focus on His place. Jesus would adjust Dr. Seuss' words to: "Oh, the place in Me, I want you to go!"

On the surface, James appears to be wandering off course in verses nine to eleven, but a closer scrutiny of these verses reveals a very important link in the chain of trials. Just like the links in a chain, there is an essential connection between each link. If we shake the chain on one end, it will create movement throughout the chain all the way to the other end. As we move the chain of trials from side to side in verses nine to eleven, we rest in **God's place** for us because we have spent time learning how to pray **God's prayer**, which is a request for wisdom to understand **God's purpose**. God's purpose becomes clearer as we see trials from **God's perspective**. This leads us to the first link of the chain which starts as we give ourselves to and release our will to **God's power**.

In verse nine, James uses a little Greek word "*de*" meaning "but" or "and." If you check, most English versions do not include "but" or "and" in their translations. However, it is a very helpful word in connecting the links in our chain of trials, not only to verse 8, but it reverberates all the way back to verse one. As already noted, James is addressing the believer, both then and now, in the throes of trials. Remember in verse one, the recipients of his letter were James' fellow Israelites facing trials because they were scattered among the Gentile nations. In verse two and again here in verse nine, James addresses the readers as brothers and sisters or as we would put it, believers in Christ. To understand what James has been communicating to us in this link of the chain (vss. 9-11), it is important that we recognize that James is addressing believers (you and me) since verse two. Here in verse nine, James again speaks directly to us by using the description of brothers and sisters. James will describe two different believers: one in humble circumstances (v.9) and one who is rich (vss. 10-11).

> "All of our possessions, possess a little of us."
>
> -Michael Card,
> Christian Musician

The believer in humble circumstances depicts a person of little significance by this world's evaluation. Instead of putting on God's lens to look at life and trials from His perspective, most individuals put on a worldview lens that values and pursues possessions, pleasures, or position. Even as believers, we put on these glasses that shades the way we look at life. The philosophy of our world tells us we need possessions for significance, so we seek possessions or the newest thing on the market. We buy things we can't afford to impress people we don't like. Our world shouts to us that we have arrived when we are at a point in our lives where we can enjoy pleasures whenever, wherever, and to what degree we want. We live in a culture of over indulgence and the home of the "supersize." There is a mindset telling us that to have position or power in our workplace, community, school, or any other arena will give us value. So, we strive to have status, demand others to respect our word and wishes, and to be esteemed as the top dog.

Not only does this search for significance slither into our thinking, but also our troubles and difficulties can rob us of significance in the estimation of others. Our trials may have left us with few material possessions, emotionally bankrupt, with physical maladies, loss of companionship, doubting ourselves, questioning God, or one of a host of other invading thoughts and emotions. I have observed that when you experience one or more of these struggles, others may look down on you, and that stings. Yes, even believers. And that stings twice as much! Disastrously, many times Christians shoot their own and eat their wounded. Not only did the "religious leaders" of His day wound Jesus; they killed Him. If you find yourself in this place, let the words of Jesus slowly cascade over you like a hot comforting shower:

> Come to me, all you who are weary and burdened, and I will give you rest. Take my yoke upon you and learn from me, for I am gentle and humble in heart, and you will find rest for your souls. For my yoke is easy and my burden is light. (Matthew 11:28-30)

Take note of how Jesus describes Himself, *"I am gentle and* **humble** *in heart."* Jesus uses the same Greek word for humble to describe Himself as James uses to describe us in humble circumstances (v.9). In the evaluation of many individuals and definitely in this world's philosophy, Jesus is of little significance. When we are placed in this group that the world sees as insignificant, let the soothing warmth of Jesus' words shower you with the comfort that we are in the company of Jesus. This is God's place for us in trials.

God's place is a place of seeming contradiction. James tells us, when we are in humble circumstances to take pride in our high position. This is not an arrogance in what we accomplish but the idea is "to boast over a privilege."[3] The privilege we have is an exalted position that comes to us because of Christ and in Christ. This "refers to the present Spiritual status which by virtue of his relation to Christ, the Christian now enjoys."[4] Commentator Douglas Moo adds, "James' point, then, is that believers must look beyond the world's evaluation to understand who they are and look at God's view of them."[5] For we who are believers, God sees our spiritual position in Christ. Not because of what we have done but because of the incredible and completed work of Jesus Christ. Later, James himself gives us insight into this place that is of little earthly significance but great eternal significance. *"Listen, my dear brothers and sisters:* **Has not God chosen those who are poor in the eyes of the world** *to be rich in faith and to inherit the kingdom he promised those who love him?" (James 2:5).* God's place for the believers in Jesus Christ may be viewed by many as a place of insignificance, but God has chosen to make us rich and give us an inheritance in His place.

As we emphasize our incredible position in Christ for dealing with trials, let us allow a few passages to soak into the fabric of our being, to renew our thinking to live in light of the reality of God's place.

- Blessed be the God and Father of our Lord Jesus Christ, **who has blessed us in Christ with every spiritual blessing in the heavenly places....** (Ephesians 1:3 ESV)

- For God wanted them [believers] to know that the riches and glory of Christ are for you Gentiles, too. And this is the secret: **Christ lives in you. This gives you assurance of sharing his glory.** (Colossians 1:27 NLT)

- But because of his great love for us, God, who is rich in mercy, made us alive with Christ even when we were dead in transgressions—it is by grace you have been saved. And God raised us up with Christ and **seated us with him in the heavenly realms in Christ Jesus....** (Ephesians 2:4-6)

  Since, then, you have been raised with Christ, set your hearts on things above, **where Christ is, seated at the right hand of God**. Set your minds on things above, not on earthly things. For you died, and your life is now hidden with Christ in God. (Colossians 3:1-3)

During the test of trials, we must focus our thoughts on the unique place we have because we are in Christ. Paul describes for us how God's great power raised Jesus Christ from the dead and seated Him at His right hand, *"I also pray that you will understand the incredible greatness of God's power for us who believe him. This is the same mighty power that raised Christ from the dead and seated him in the place of honor at God's right hand in the heavenly realms"* (Ephesians 1:19-20 NLT). We are placed in Christ and according to Ephesians 2:4-6, noted above, we are seated with Christ in the heavenly realms. This is how God sees us! We are placed in Christ and Christ is seated at the right hand of the Father. The chair we sit in is next to the Father at His right hand. This is God's place for us. Because this is how God sees us, it becomes a critical change in the way we think about our relationship with the Father. It is not a place of condemnation but a place of freedom as Paul so magnificently describes in Romans 8:1-2 (ESV), *"There is therefore now no condemnation for those who are in Christ Jesus. For the law of the Spirit of life has set you free in Christ Jesus from the law of sin and death."* Not only does James tell us to see our trials from God's perspective (v.2), but trials are a reminder to view ourselves in the place God sees us and to be thankful for our spiritual identity in Christ. Though many may not give much significance to our "humble place," we can praise God for the exalted place we have in Christ, seated at the right hand of the Father. It is a place of honor. It is God's place.

James gives us this imperative to "boast" so that we would emphasize two very practical applications in the battle of trials. First, praise God for the incredible place we have in Jesus Christ. Second, continually focus our thoughts on how God sees us in Christ, seated at His right hand. God's place for us is the significance we have because of Christ's work and because we have been placed in Christ, the hope of glory. This is God's place for the believer. **Hold tightly to our place in Christ during the test of trials!**

GODLY BOASTING

"This is what the LORD says:
'Don't let the wise boast in their wisdom,
or the powerful boast in their power,
or the rich boast in their riches.
But **those who wish to boast
should boast in this alone:
that they truly know me
and understand that I am the** LORD
who demonstrates unfailing love
and who brings justice
and righteousness to the earth,
and that I delight in these things.
I, the LORD, have spoken!'"

Jeremiah 9:23-25 (NLT)

God's Place for Us in Trials is to Hold Loosely to Our Position on Earth.   James 1:10-11

Once again, James uses the little Greek word "*de*," meaning "but" or "and," to link verse nine with verses nine to eleven. James is contrasting two believers. Let the brother in humble circumstance boast in the fact that he is lifted to a high position in Christ, but (*de*) let the brother who is rich boast in his humble position. As in verse 9, James' writing seems to be a contradiction. However, we discover the humble position depicts a person of little significance (not just in wealth) by this world's evaluation, whereas, the rich person depicts a person of great significance by this world's evaluation. Again, Moo's comments are helpful to put the cookies on the bottom shelf for us to easily reach and consume. "If the one who is rich is a Christian, then James' encouragement to that person to take pride in his low position will mean that the rich believer is to boast not in his wealth or his elevated social position, but in his identification with Christ and his people, a matter of 'humiliation' (low position) in the eyes of the world."[6]

We find many examples of godly, wealthy individuals in Scripture. Abraham, Job, David, King Solomon, Joseph of Arimathea, Lydia of Thyatira, and Philemon are a few that come to mind. Wealth, in and of itself, is not the problem but riches do seem to present a unique and sometimes strong deterrent to trusting in Christ and resting in God's place. In Luke's gospel, he gives us the account of the rich ruler who asked Jesus what he need to do to inherit eternal life. Jesus knew the ruler relied on his status of wealth but did not trust in God. Always going to the heart of the matter, Jesus asked him about keeping the commandments, and the ruler said he had. It is not as much a statement of pride on the ruler's part, as it was his assessment of himself. It would be excellent if we could say the same thing, but keeping the commandments is not what God requires for salvation or to be in His place. Luke gives us an unsuspecting twist in the account:

> When Jesus heard this, he said to him, "You still lack one thing. Sell everything you have and give to the poor, and you will have treasure in heaven. Then come, follow me." When he heard this, he became very sad, because he was very wealthy. Jesus looked at him and said, "How hard it is for the rich to enter the kingdom of God!" (Luke 18:22-24)[7]

> *"Pride gets no pleasure out of having something, only out of having more of it than the next person. We say that people are proud of being rich, or clever, or good-looking, but they are not. They are proud of being richer, or cleverer, or better-looking than others. If everyone became equally rich, or clever, or good-looking there would be nothing to be proud about... It is the comparison that makes you proud: the pleasure of being above the rest. Once the element of competition is gone, pride is gone."*
>
> -C.S. Lewis
> *Mere Christianity*[8]

It wasn't that Jesus did not want this ruler in heaven. It wasn't that the ruler had to do something to attain salvation, like ridding himself of his riches. Jesus addressed the ruler's problem. He placed his significance on his earthly position, and it kept him from God's place. (In several passages, James warns us of the problems and troubles associated with wealth: 2:5-7; 4:13-17; 5:1-6.) Status that is valued in the eyes of this world, whether it be possessions, pleasures, or position, are transitory in nature, and as believers they keep us from seeing ourselves in and living in God's place.

The story is told of a very wealthy man who received the news that he only had three months to live. He came home from the doctor's visit and told his wife he was going to figure out a way to take his money with him when he died. He gave it considerable thought and concluded that he would liquidate his investments and take all his money out of the bank. His plan was to place the money in bags in his attic, and then he could grab the bags of money on his way to heaven. So, that's what he did. In time, the man passed away. After a period of mourning, the man's wife thought it was time to move forward with her life. She thought the best way would be to give the house a thorough cleaning and purging. She would begin in the attic and work her way to the basement. As the widow began the project, a friend graciously volunteered to help her. Upon entering the attic, the ladies found all the bags of money the rich man had placed there. The man's wife said to her friend, "I knew he should have put some of the bags in the basement." All earthly wealth and status is temporal, but our wealth and status in Christ is eternal.

In verse ten, the word used for low position is the same word used for humble in verse nine. It is also the same word that Jesus uses to describe Himself when He says, "I am gentle and **humble** in heart" (Matthew 11:29). Because of its importance, it is worth another look. As with many of his topics, James circles back around and gives us a fresh look at the topic from another angle. In chapter 4 verse 6, James quotes from the book of Proverbs when he says, *"But he gives us more grace. That is why Scripture says: "God opposes the proud but shows favor to the humble."* This is God's place for us. As believers in Jesus Christ, we are salmon swimming against the stream of our human nature, our culture, and temporal values. God is telling us that when we are proud, He is in opposition to us because Jesus is "humble in heart." When we are humble, we find grace in God's place.

Peter, in his letter, also quotes this verse from Proverbs, but he adds a powerful comment, *"Therefore humble yourselves under the mighty hand of God, that He may exalt you at the proper time..."*

(1 Peter 5:6, NASB). The word Peter uses for exalt is the same one James uses for high position (v.9). This high position we have in Christ will be fully realized and enjoyed one day and forever in heaven. But for now, God is at work to make us humble and uses trials to help us understand God's place for us. This one thing we can be certain of: God is at work to make all of us humble. We can humble ourselves or God can humble us. We don't like either method, but humbling ourselves is always the better road to take. It is like changing the oil in our car. We can change it every few thousand miles, or we can change it when the oil burns out causing damage to the motor. You can change it now or you can change it later, but you will change it.

James gives us three motivating factors as reasons for us to focus on our position in Christ, God's place in dealing with the test of trials. **First, the temporary nature of life is an incentive to focus on Christ.** James 1:10b states, *"because the one who values earthly things will pass away."* The words "will pass away" mean to cease to exist or disappear.[9] James' own words

LIFE IS HARD

Yet man is born to trouble as surely as sparks fly upward.

Job 5:7

LIFE IS SHORT

Man born of woman is of few days and full of trouble.

Job 14:1

speak to the fact that life is short, *"How do you know what your life will be like tomorrow? Your life is like the morning fog—it's here a little while, then it's gone"* (James 4:14 NLT).

Second, the troubled nature of life illustrates the need to focus on Christ. James 1:11a, *"For the sun rises"* begins the illustration of the flower's demise. This illustration paints a picture of our lives. In the portrait, we see the heat of the sun and a scorching east wind. It is the same vivid colors of the word picture used to illustrate our good friend Jonah. His shade was suddenly taken away, and the sun and hot wind assaulted him, *"When the sun rose, God appointed a scorching east wind, and the sun beat down on the head of Jonah so that he was faint. And he asked that he might die and said, 'It is better for me to die than to live'"* (Jonah 4:8 ESV). We can relate to Jonah when we experience the intense heat of our trials, we want relief from our challenges, and sometimes we might feel the only escape from our tests is the end of our lives. James continues to paint this picture of the flower, and his brushstrokes reveal an image of a withered flower. Its leaves have fallen from the stem, and its majesty has ceased to exist. This illustration of the flower serves to motivate us to hold loosely the values of this world in the midst of our trials and to hold tightly to the values we have in Christ.

Third, the transitory nature of life inevitably motives us to focus on Christ. James uses the phrase, *"In the same way,"* in 1:11b to associate us with the depiction of the flower just given. We are born, bloom as humans, fade in age, and die, simply as we go through life, or as James puts it, *"as he goes about his business."* This is a snapshot of a person who only focuses on the here and now. We "will fade away" is a statement of fact that is yet in the future but is certain to come. It describes for us a withering or wasting away. The older we get the more we relate to what James is saying, as our bodies and minds begin to wither like the flower. "The picture of the rich 'withering' continues the simile of the fading flower: the verb is picturesque and may be used of the dying of a flower or the decaying of plants like roses as well as ears of corn. The reference is to the loss of riches and earthly prosperity, not to eternal destiny."[10]

Motivating Factors to Focus on Our Place in Christ:

1. The temporary nature of life is an incentive to focus on Christ.

2. The troubled nature of life illustrates our need to focus on Christ.

3. The transitory nature of life inevitably motives us to focus on Christ.

One day at work, I was having a conversation with a co-worker. I stated, "I'm ready to go. I just wasn't planning on going today." Her response was, "Don't say that!" She didn't want to talk about or even think of death. The end of our life here on earth can be a difficult discussion and an unpleasant thought, but James gives us these motivating reasons so we will not cling to our earthly status but cherish our eternal status. Sometimes we become too comfortable with this world and lose focus on the one to come with our Lord Jesus Christ. My heart breaks for my co-worker, because her significance in the trials of life are in the values of this temporal world. She has not come to saving faith in Jesus Christ nor grasped what she would be in Christ, God's place. My question is "Have you?" If you have not, would you pray this simple prayer of faith from your heart:

> *"God, I know that my life is short. I admit I have sinned against you but right now, I put my trust in Jesus Christ for my eternal position and destiny. I ask Jesus to come into my life to be my Lord and Savior. Thank you for doing that and for putting me in Christ, Your place. Amen."*

If you have come to saving faith in Jesus Christ, you may want to pray something like this:

> *"Father, thank you for walking with me through the trials of life. Thank you that Jesus has done all the work for my salvation, and there is nothing I can do to deserve or achieve it. As a believer, I know that you view me as in Christ at Your right hand. Please give me a breathtaking understanding of what it means to be in Your place. Father, forgive me for holding tightly to earthly things, and help me to hold tightly to eternal things. Please give me what I need in the tests of my trials to focus clearly on Your place and to look casually at earthly values. In Jesus' name, Amen."*

A Passport from Heaven

It is always fun to look at my passports and see the stamps I received from various countries. As I look at the stamps from the countries: Israel, the Philippines, Singapore, Amsterdam-Holland, Tanzania, Zambia, Bahamas, and others, they bring back a lot of good memories. Each time I travel outside of the United States of America, I have tasted unusual foods, encountered foreign languages or accents, experienced different cultural norms, witnessed unique clothing, and saw beautiful and historical sites. On the other hand, I obviously stood out as a foreigner from the USA by my dress, speech, actions, and looks. There were times during my travels when I enjoyed a foreign country so much I didn't want to leave. Sometimes I became so attached to that country with the friendships made, the new experiences, and the status given, that home was just an afterthought. On the other hand, whether it was ten days or three months, a time would come when I would begin to miss the USA, my home. Sometimes my thoughts would migrate back home, and I would struggle to keep focused on tasks I was there to accomplish. It seems the best mental state is somewhere between.

On the front of my passports, it says "United States of America" to show my citizenship. Though I did not have to receive a stamp upon returning to the States, because this is my home, I always try to get a USA stamp. As I go through the airports, I notice others with passports. Their passports may be a different color, and on the front the passport has the name of the country in which that individual is a citizen. As I reflect on living out God's place in our day to day life, I compare it to traveling to another country. As a believer, the front of our passport identifies our citizenship; it says, "Heaven." This is clearly declared in Philippians 3:20, *"But **our citizenship is in heaven**. And we eagerly await a Savior from there, the Lord Jesus Christ."* At times we get too entrenched in earthly matters, evaluating ourselves by material standards, not spiritual. We forget that we are citizens of another country. We lose focus of the fact that the trials of this life should lead us to God's place in Christ.

As I described in my travels to foreign countries, there always seemed to be a time when my thoughts and longings became so great for home that I lost sight of why I was there. When we focus on God's place, we must be aware of the other side of the coin also and alert to the spiritual battle. As long as we have breath on this earth, God is at work in us and through us. We can say with confidence this includes our trials and challenges, but our focus is to be on our heavenly home. However, it has been said that *"Christians can be so heavenly minded that we are no earthly good."* Continue to be faithful to what God is asking of us during our times of trials. Paul's words give us guidance and encouragement as he shares how he wrestled with this very issue in Philippians 1:21-26:

> For to me, to live is Christ and to die is gain. If I am to go on living in the body, this will mean fruitful labor for me. Yet what shall I choose? I do not know! **I am torn between the two**: I desire to depart and be with Christ, which is better by far; but it is more necessary for you that I remain in the body. Convinced of this, I know that I will remain, and I will continue with all of you for your progress and joy in the faith, so that through my being with you again your boasting in Christ Jesus will abound on account of me.

What great riches we have in Christ! Focusing on God's place will bring a radical change in us to hold loosely to the temporal values of this world and tightly to our eternal treasures in Christ. This is not an easy transformation. Because to live this way is counter-culture and contrary to our nature, we live in tension. When we see ourselves as God sees us, trials will take on a new significance. While here on earth, we realize He is working to have us live as He views us and to recognize God is developing us for eternity. Now, we do not fully enjoy or understand God's place for us, but one day in Christ's presence we will. The day we will forever be in Christ's presence is the day we long for and reveals God's promise to us in our trials. James magnificently shows us the hope that accompanies the trials we encounter. Let's look together at this hope we have as James will now outline God's promise during our test of trials.

DOESN'T MY TEACHER GRADE ON A CURVE?

Letting our trials lead us to God's Place; James 1:9-11

-Think About It & Talk About It-

1. Describe a teacher you had that reminds you of Dr. Bartlett. Why do we want to think that God grades on a curve? Why is it dangerous to think about God in this way?

2. The believer in **humble** circumstance depicts a person of little significance by this world's evaluation. This same word for **humble** is used by:

    ➢ Jesus – *"I am gentle and **humble** in heart" (Matthew 11:29)*

    ➢ James – *"God opposes the proud but shows favor to the **humble**" (James 4:6)*

    ➢ Peter – *"**Humble** yourselves under the mighty hand of God" (1 Peter 5:9)*

    What do these usages of the word humble teach you about God's Place?

3. In this chapter four passages were emphasized to help you understand your position in Christ: Ephesians 1:3; Colossians 1:27; Ephesians 2:4-6; Colossians 3:1-3. Which passage best helps you understand your position in Christ? Why? How does that passage change your thinking in regard to the test of trials?

4. James gives us three motivating factors to focus on our Place in Christ and hold loosely to the things of earth. Which one motives you right now? Explain.

   ➢ The temporary nature of life is an incentive to focus on Christ.

   ➢ The troubled nature of life illustrates our need to focus on Christ.

   ➢ The transitory nature of life inevitably motives us to focus on Christ

5. Describe a time you went on a trip and felt like you never want to come home. Describe a time you went on a trip and couldn't wait to get home. How can your experience help you understand and live for God's Place? How can you focus on your position in Christ and still be the ambassador for Christ on earth God wants you to be?

Chapter 6

I'M BEING RECOGNIZED AT THE AWARDS' CEREMONY?!

Remembering Our Trials Have God's Promise

James 1:12

"But isn't it wrong to be motivated by reward? No, it isn't. If it were wrong, Christ wouldn't offer it to us as a motivation. Reward is His idea, not ours."

-Randy Alcorn, *The Treasure Principle*[1]

School Awards and Recognitions

The end of the school year brings a nervous excitement. The rigors of exams, assignments, and going to class give way to the anticipation of the warm, carefree days of summer. As the school year closes, and at other times through the school year, we find events such as award ceremonies or sports banquets. Recognition and awards bring their own sense of anticipation and accomplishment. Will my work be recognized? Have I done enough to merit an award? Will the green-eyed monster of jealousy whisper in my ear as my classmates, teammates, and friends receive recognition? Will I be surprised by an award? Perhaps, I don't really care about the awards and recognitions that are being given. Whatever image runs through our heads, it is nice to receive an award and recognition.

Regardless of any award or recognition they receive, my wife and I are extremely proud of each of our three boys and grateful to God for entrusting them to us. As parents, we have received numerous notifications that one of our children is being recognized or given an award. It may be a character award, an academic award, or an athletic recognition. The notification is to provide information about the event so we can make arrangements to attend the event. On one particular occasion, when our son was notified he was receiving an award, his response was something like our chapter title, "I'm getting recognized at the Awards' Ceremony?!" Simultaneously, he made a statement and asked a question. He had not given thought to his academic accomplishments, so he stated he did not know what award or awards he might be receiving. He had not focused on the awards, so he questioned the credibility of receiving one. The Awards' Ceremony came, and true to the school's word and in spite of his impressions, our son was recognized for more than one academic achievement.

Just like the school, God notifies believers of several crowns we might receive. As James continues his treatment of the topic of trials, he makes us aware of the crown of life in verse 12. God has promised this crown to those who love Him and pass the test of trials. Paul gives us a glimpse into receiving crowns, *"For we must all stand before Christ to be judged. We will each receive whatever we deserve for the good or evil we have done in this earthly body"* (2 Corinthians 5:10 NLT).

> *"Life is like a coin. You can spend it any way you want, but you can only spend it once."*
>
> -Ben Siaki
> *Missionary*

Admittedly, there is more discussion and debate concerning the events of the judgment seat of Christ than we can or will cover. For our purposes, we want to focus on the rewards given for how we lived our life here on earth. We must be quick to make this important note: we are not saved by good works but unto good works as Paul makes perfectly clear when he makes one of the most magnificent proclamations in the Scriptures: *"For it is by grace you have been saved, through faith—and this is not from yourselves, it is the gift of God— not by works, so that no one can boast. For we are God's handiwork, created in Christ Jesus to do good works, which God prepared in advance for us to do"* (Ephesians 2:8-10).

Even more than a school or a person, God keeps His promises. Each believer in Jesus Christ will stand at the judgment seat of Christ. As we stand before the Lord Jesus, we may receive a crown we didn't expect. We may receive a crown with humble jubilation. But rest assured, Jesus Christ will keep His promise regarding the test of trials.

Let us examine what James says in V.12 about overcoming life's challenges. We pass the test of trials by remembering our trials have God's promise. God's promise in trials reveals two principles for us: 1) God's promise is a blessing, when we persevere under our trials; 2) God's promise is a reward, when we prove our faith is genuine through our trials.

God's Promise is a Blessing, When We Persevere under Our Trials. James 1:12a

Blessed is the one who perseveres under trial
because, having stood the test,
that person will receive the crown of life…

James 1:12a

We have come to the last stop on our safari through the jungle called, "Trials." Before we disembark, we pause to reflect on the previous checkpoints. At the first three: God's Power, God's Perspective, and God's Purpose, we look from God's observation tower to see our trials as He sees them. At the last three: God's Prayer, God's Place, and God's Promise, we look from our observation tower to see God's desire for our response to life's trials.

"Blessed is the one who perseveres under trial..." This word for blessed is the same word we find in the Beatitudes section of the Sermon on the Mount. A quick glance at the Beatitudes (Matthew 5:3-12) shows they dovetail with what James is saying about trials. Both Jesus and James reveal that difficulties bring a blessing or "spiritual happiness." To understand what God describes as blessed or happy we want to dig into the Greek word used by both Jesus and James, *makarios*. This way we will understand the word "blessed" with the meaning that God gives it and intends for us to have. Blessed means "to be pronounced or declared happy." "It carries the idea of profound inner, joy and satisfaction, a joy that only the Lord Himself is able to bestow on those who, for His sake and in His power, faithfully and patiently endure and conquer trials."[2] Interestingly, we find the word joy making a resurgence to the forefront. The perspective of joy is brought into focus.

> **Blessed**
>
> *"to be pronounced or declared happy."*

In order to help us grasp the biblical idea of blessed, we can think in terms of a graduation or a wedding. When an individual graduates from school, he or she generally attends a commencement ceremony. That individual enters the ceremony as a non-graduate, but upon receiving his or her diploma, there is a "declaration" that this person is now a graduate of the school he or she attended. There can be happiness, joy, sadness or even indifference, but regardless of the emotion, that individual is declared a graduate. It is a statement of fact.

A wedding ceremony can also illustrate the God's meaning of blessed. Before the wedding ceremony, they arrive as two single individuals and leave a married couple. They may not feel any different, but the declaration is a description of who they are now.

James tells us that when we let the test of trials do its work, we are declared or pronounced "happy" in God's eyes. The trials have been difficult, we may not be where we wanted to be, and our emotions may not be "happy" but from God's viewpoint, we are declared spiritually happy. This gives us a firmer grasp of the concept of joy in trials. For many of us this is a change in our thinking, a shift in our paradigm, because we associate happiness with no problems, no pain, and doing whatever we please. In fact, as parents, many times we perpetuate this thinking in our children when we say, "I just want you to be happy." Are we asking for them to have trials, because when they persevere, they will be declared happy in God's eyes? Undoubtedly, that is not exactly what we are meaning. Let God's definition and value challenge us to rethink what it means to be happy, at least declared happy in God's eyes.

> *"God is a sure paymaster, though He does not always pay at the end of every week."*
>
> -Charles Spurgeon

We persevere by remaining under our trials until they accomplish their purpose; this is when we receive God's promise of blessing. James takes us back to verses three and four when we discovered the testing of our faith produces perseverance. Perseverance does its work so that we will be complete and mature in Christ. Remember, the idea is to remain under our trials. Perseverance or endurance is what we would call "stick-to-it-ness." We stay with the trial until it accomplishes God's purpose for us, even when we don't fully understand or like what God is doing. This is when we find "spiritual happiness."

Remember our definition: *a trial is a test God uses to prove the genuineness of our faith and to develop our maturity in Jesus Christ.* James addresses the second half of our definition in verse 12a. We are declared happy or blessed in the mind of God when we continue to hang in there under difficult trials until they produce spiritual completeness and maturity in us. This is God's promise of blessing for us in our trials. Let this important change be a challenge to the usual way we think about trials and to think new, different, and godly thoughts in the face of trials.

God's Promise is a Reward, When We Prove Our Faith is Genuine through Our Trials. James 1:12b

*Blessed is the one who perseveres under trial **because, having stood the test, that person will receive the crown of life that the Lord has promised to those who love him**.*

James 1:12

*"Blessed is the man who perseveres under trial, **because**..."* Not only does James speak to us about God's promise of a

blessing, but now he uses the word "because" to declare three reasons why God's promise is a reward. As he articulates the reasons, James shines additional light on the first part of our definition, *a trial is a test that God uses to prove the genuineness of our faith.* James connects the dots for us between the relationship of God's purpose in trials which he discussed in verse 3a, *"because you know that the testing of your faith"* and God's promise of reward in verse 12b, *"because, having stood the test, that person will receive the crown of life that the Lord has promised to those who love him."* Let's examine these reasons one at a time taking special care to note the challenge for our daily lives associated with each one.

First, God's reward is given to those whose faith is genuine, so prove it now! The word here in verse twelve is the same one from verse three, *dokimos,* which we learned means "to test or prove the genuineness of something." When we have stood the test literally means "having become approved." When our faith is validated through the test of trials, we receive notification for the awards' ceremony. We encounter many different sizes, shapes, and colors of trials that ambush us and splatter us like a polka dots as we walk the sidewalks of life. The tests of trials occur in our homes, schools, workplaces, and communities where God wants us to demonstrate that the faith is our own. This is why we have mental, physical, emotional, relational, and spiritual tests: to prove our faith is real. Today is the day to pass the test of trials and demonstrate to the Lord our faith is genuine. Just like awards ceremonies and recognition assemblies, they come after the work is done, so our spiritual rewards take place after the work is complete. For the crown of life, it is reward in the future after our work on earth is done. Because the future reward seems so far away, and the difficulties of proving our faith are right now, we might falter or want to quit. But Paul gives us a peek about the quality of our work now being tested by a future fire. This glimpse is to encourage us to keep on keeping on.

> For no one can lay any foundation other than the one already laid, which is Jesus Christ. If anyone builds on this foundation using gold, silver, costly stones, wood, hay or straw, their work will be shown for what it is, because the Day will bring it to light. It will be revealed with fire, and the fire will test the quality of each person's work. If what has been built survives, the builder will receive a reward. If it is burned up, the builder will suffer loss but yet will be saved— even though only as one escaping through the flames (1 Corinthians 3:11-15).

Second, God's reward is given in the future, so persevere now! James' words inform us the reward is yet to come: *"he will receive the crown of life."* We do not know when this giving of the crown of life will happen. We want the reward even before the trial. As someone once said, "Instant gratification takes too long." In the testing of our faith, we are asked to persevere, endure, to have stick-to-it-ness. Words we love to hate. As we endure the tests of trials, remember as believers we are called to be faithful; *"Moreover, it is required of stewards that they be found faithful"* (1 Corinthians 4:2 ESV). This crown of life resurfaces when Jesus gives this injunction to suffering Christians in the book of Revelation. Jesus emphasizes that we persevere now, because the reward is still future. "Remain faithful even to the point of death, and I will give you the crown that is life itself" (Revelation 2:10b NET).

Third, God's reward is given to those who love God, so obey Him now! What amazingly powerful, humbling, and daunting words! The crown of life is given to those who love Jesus! James' comments about this reward will compel us to look again at what he stated in chapter 2 verse 5, *"Listen, my dear brothers and sisters: Has not God chosen those who are poor in the eyes of the world to be rich in faith and to inherit the kingdom he promised those who love him?"* God has chosen those who are insignificant in the eyes of this world and do not measure up to the standards of this world. We understand, this is God's place for us in Christ. God chose us, has

> Jesus replied: "Love the Lord your God with all your heart and with all your soul and with all your mind."
>
> Matthew 22:37

made us rich in faith, and has given us the inheritance of His kingdom. Once again, James describes for us the tremendous position we have in Christ.

James has been methodically putting together a puzzle for us, and now every piece is tightly interlocking to bring the picture of the first twelve verses together. These pieces of God's power, perspective, purpose, prayer, place, and promise now form a message of love to Jesus Christ. James connects these pieces in such a way as to strengthen and build our love for Jesus, so our lives will shout, "Jesus, I love You!" The ones receiving this great promise are the ones loving Jesus. Jesus said the greatest commandment is to love God with all we have, but I would venture to say that we struggle with "how do I tell or show Jesus I love

Him?" Jesus, being true to His character, didn't keep us in the dark. Jesus shoots straight with us, **"If you love me, you will keep my commandments"** (John 14:15 ESV). "Jesus replied, **'Anyone who loves me will obey my teaching.** My Father will love them, and we will come to them and make our home with them'" (John 14:23).

John, one of Jesus' twelve disciples, records these words of Jesus in his gospel: "if you love Me keep My commandments." John gives us valuable additional insight in his first epistle about loving Jesus, *"In fact, this is love for God: to keep his commands. And his commands are not burdensome"* (1 John 5:3). John reiterates the fact that we love God by keeping His commands, then he tells us these commands are not a burden. The word John uses for burdensome "suggests the idea of a heavy and oppressive burden."[3] There is a tension in us because if we are brutally honest, each of us would say at least some of the time that God's commands feel like a heavy, oppressive burden. But John just told us that what God is asking us to do in keeping His commands is NOT a heavy burden.

> *"Closeness to God is not about feelings. It's about obedience. ... I don't know how you feel close to God. And no one I know who seems to be close to God knows anything about those feelings either. I know if we obey, occasionally the feeling follows. Not always, but occasionally. I know that if we disobey, we don't have a shot at it."*
>
> - Rich Mullins
> *Musician*

Let us step back from the table where we have been putting together the pieces of James' puzzle so we can see the whole picture and how the pieces he has joined dovetail with John's. Remember, Jesus expressed powerful words of comfort and strength, when He said if we are weary and burdened to come to Him and He would give us rest (review Matthew 11:28-30). Many of us are so battle worn and fatigued right now in the spiritual fight that to demonstrate our love only adds weight to our already heavy backpack. Jesus said He was humble in heart, the same place He wants us to be. By stepping back from the puzzle, we see that the very first principle James gave us now snugly fits with this puzzle piece. We pass the test of trials by yielding our trials to God's Power. When we try in our own strength to obey God's commands, they are heavy and oppressive, because we cannot carry them! But by yielding to Jesus as the Master and Controller of our lives, what God asks of us is not a burden; it is an expression of love.

By making a lifetime commitment to serving Jesus Christ, we plug into His power and God gives us the strength, joy, and ability to obey His commands. One of God's great characteristics is that He will never ask us to do something that He will not enable us to do. Because the Christian life is impossible, and Jesus was the only one who lived it perfectly, He left the Holy Spirit to reside within us and give us the ability to yield to Jesus as the Master and Controller of our lives. Remember, victory in the Christian life comes through surrender. Surrender to the only One who can give us what we need in times of trials to say and show Jesus, **"Jesus, I love you!"**

If we want to tell Jesus "I love You" or demonstrate our love for Jesus, we do what He says in His Word. How does all this fit with trials? Simply, we are put in the position of a test of our faith to see if we will live out our faith in that trial. By living our faith in even the smallest, most mundane, seemingly insignificant events in our lives, we prove our faith is real and tell Jesus we love Him. This is a major shift in the way we look at trials, and we need to begin now to make this change as we face the test of trials. They are not problems to avoid, crises to endure, tests to pass; they are expressions of our love for our Savior Jesus Christ. When yielded to Him, we can find joy in the trial and strength to obey. Right now, each of us is staring into the eyes of a trial, a testing of our faith. We know what God wants us to do about it, so without further delay obey. Take this precious opportunity to tell Jesus, "I love you!"

God's Rewards

1. God's reward is given to those whose faith is genuine, so prove it now!

2. God's reward is given in the future, so persevere now!

3. God's reward is given to those who love God, so obey Him now!

The Raymond A. Templeton Award

Most people are familiar with the Nobel Peace Prize named after Alfred Nobel. It is given to those who preserve, promote, or progress peace. Many are familiar with the Cy Young Award named after the great Hall of Fame baseball pitcher Cy Young. Two Cy Young Awards are given each year in Major League Baseball, one to the best pitcher in the American League and one to the best pitcher in the National League. Some are familiar with the Antoinette Perry Award for Excellence in Broadway Theatre or better known as The Tony Awards named after Antoinette "Tony" Perry. The Tony Awards recognize excellence in live Broadway theatre and are given at an annual ceremony in New York City. Probably no one reading these words is familiar with The Raymond A. Templeton Award named after Raymond Templeton. The Award was given to the graduating senior at Raymond Templeton's High School that best demonstrated the character qualities Raymond possessed both on and off the athletic field or court.

Raymond Templeton loved sports, but he was not able to compete in athletics. He was on the academic honor roll but did not graduate from high school. He was kind to everyone, but a disease was cruel to him. He was smaller and weaker than other students but had a bigger and stronger faith than most. His life on earth ended during high school, but Raymond's impact continues to live.

As Raymond walked the halls of our Christian school, I sensed something unique about him. In the setting where God placed Raymond, in the midst of his physical trials, he exhibited an unwavering faith by allowing Christ to give him joy and acceptance.

Though it was a Christian school, some students were not Christians, and some of the Christians did not live for the Lord. A few of the Christians lived out their faith, but Raymond shone like a bright star on the darkest night. Raymond took the role of the manager for the basketball team, while his brother took the role of the star player. His character of Christlikeness continued to be exhibited as he took delight in and not envy of his brother's success. As Raymond handed out towels and gave water to the basketball players, his demeanor was reminiscent of Jesus taking a towel and a basin of water to wash the feet of the disciples. Raymond was about three years older than me, and it was my great privilege to know him, though it was brief.

In the years that followed his passing, an award was established in Raymond's name. The Raymond A. Templeton award went to the senior athlete who best exhibited Christ's character while performing well on the athletic field or court, the same qualities Raymond daily strove to communicate in the way he lived and would certainly have spilled onto the athletic field.

During my senior year, the time came to recognize and give awards to the athletes at the school's annual Sports Banquet. My mind raced like a hamster on its wheel. My palms were sweaty with nervous anticipation. Who would be the Raymond A. Templeton Award winner for my class? Would it, could it, should it be me? I hoped but didn't want to be prideful. I thought I had demonstrated Christ in my athletic competitions, but others in my class could be just as qualified. Pride and not considering others; now those were not traits of Raymond and definitely not of Christ. So I waited and wondered if I had demonstrated Christ-likeness to the point of receiving the award, much like we wait and wonder about the crown of life. When the time came to make known that year's Raymond A. Templeton Award, I heard my name announced.

I was and still am very humbled by the selection. I do not share this story to draw attention to myself but to draw similarities to the crown of life or any reward we receive from the Lord Jesus Christ. I personally knew and observed Raymond, so I understood the character qualities his award represented. I personally know and allow Jesus to be involved in my life and want to let His character qualities be represented in me. Raymond's family wanted the award to go to someone who continued to live the life Raymond desired to live. I am a part of the family of God, and He wants me to let the world know I belong to Jesus, represent my heavenly family, and live the life Jesus wants. In a small way, I reflected and characterized Raymond's life, so I too want to reflect and characterize the Savior. As I played sports my senior year, I did not play for the purpose of winning the Raymond A. Templeton award. I simply portrayed who I was on the field and court. I do not live just to receive a crown but to be who the Lord Jesus wants me to be and leave the awarding of rewards in His nail-scarred hands. I cherish the Raymond A. Templeton Award, but the award is not about me; it is about remembering the life and character of Raymond Templeton.

The limits of our human comprehension will not allow us to imagine what it will be like to receive the crown of life or any reward the Lord gives us. But it is not about us, it is about reflecting the life and character of our Lord and Savior Jesus Christ. As we weave all of our thoughts together in the next chapter, we draw inspiration from a couple of individuals who have faced the test of trials. Along with them, let the mission of our lives be the same as John the Baptist, *"He must become greater and greater, and I must become less and less"* (John 3:30 NLT).

I'M BEING RECOGNIZED AT
THE AWARDS CEREMONY!?
Remember Our Trials Have God's Promise; James 1:12

-Think About It & Talk About It-

1. What is an award or recognition you are proud of? Is there an award or recognition you did not receive but felt you should have?

A trial is a test God uses to prove the genuineness of our faith and to develop our maturity in Jesus Christ.

2. James has given us six principles to deal with the test of trials: God's Power, God's Perspective, God's Purpose, God's Prayer, God's Place, and God's Promise. Explain how each of these principles are intertwined with each other. How do the first five principles tie into this sixth principle of God's Promise?

3. James 1:12a says, *"Blessed is the man who perseveres under trials."* What does the word "blessed" mean? How does this impact your thinking about trials? What does this part of James 1:12 add to our understanding of trials?

4. James 1:12b says, *"...because when he has stood the test, he will receive the crown of life..."* What does it mean to stand the test? What is the promised reward? What does this part of James 1:12, add to our understanding of trials?

5. God's Promise of the crown of life is given to those who love Jesus. How did Jesus tell us we show Him, "I love You?" (see John 14:15; 14:23). Explain why God's commands are **not** a burden. When and how do God's commands become a burden? The focus of James 1:1-12 is dealing with the test of trials. What are three specific ways we can let Jesus know we love Him as we seek to pass the test of trials?

THE COMMENCEMENT ADDRESS

"Christian, remember the goodness of God
in the frost of adversity."

–Charles H. Spurgeon

The Commencement Address of a Phrase

The opening of my email caused my jaw to drop hard and fast, hitting my desk with such force that the loud thud reverberated for a three block radius. The rubbing of my jaw for comfort quickly gave way to the rubbing of my eyes in disbelief. I had recently completed the opportunity of a lifetime to travel to the Nassau Theological College in Tanzania to teach a two week block-course on the book of Hebrews. Not only did I teach an eager group of seniors, but I had the honor to visit each of my students in their homes, see the world's largest lake - Lake Victoria, and take a safari through the Serengeti Game Park. But now before me was the privilege of a lifetime. In the email was an invitation by that same senior class for me to return to give their commencement address! The excitement I experienced was like the anticipation of a five year old awakening on Christmas morning. The expectation of the event soon gave way to the reality of the graduation as I travelled 10,000 miles from home to give the commencement address.

The day came for the graduation ceremony, and I was awestruck. The graduation was held on the grounds of the Nassau Theological College in the open air. It was truly a festive occasion with bright, cheerful colors and lovely, delightful decorations. Even in the heat, men were dressed in suit and tie and women in their Sunday best. The little village of Bulima was the home to the college, and many of the villagers attended the ceremony, even staying for the scrumptious post-graduation feast.

This was a remarkable once-in-a-lifetime privilege to speak to the graduates, faculty, staff, family, friends, and villagers, but what great nuggets of wisdom did I have to offer in a commencement address? Commencement means a point at which something begins. These students were beginning ministries, possibly post graduate studies, a new chapter in their lives, but most of all they were leaving behind their formal lessons and beginning to put those lessons to work in the realities of everyday life and ministry. We too have learned our lessons. The lessons of the classroom have given us the skills we need to pass the test of daily trials. Today, we commence or begin to live them out as we face mental, physical, spiritual, relational, and emotional challenges in our homes, schools, workplaces, churches, and communities.

My commencement address to you is the same phrase I gave to my Tanzanian students, **"Mtafute Mungu Kwanza!"** This is Swahili for **"Seek God First!"** Begin today to "Seek" by looking to Jesus as the pursuit of your life. Begin today to "Seek God" by loving Jesus as the passion of your life. Begin today to "Seek God First" by letting Jesus be the priority of your life.

The Commencement Address of a Principle

In the classroom at school, we may concern ourselves only with the material that will be on the final in order to pass the course. In the classroom of life, God is concerned with our learning and developing in order complete His work in us. Because God's heartbeat is for us to reflect Jesus in every character quality and

---

If you falter in a time of trouble, how small is your strength!

Proverbs 24:10

---

area of our lives, He brings the test of trials over and over. This is not only for us to pass the test but to change us into the man or woman Christ wants us to be. As we leave James' classroom to commence living in everyday situations and walk the pathways of life, let us review the principles our teacher provides for us on how to pass the test of trials.

> **We pass the test of trials by yielding our trials to God's power.**
> **We pass the test of trials by seeing our trials from God's perspective.**
> **We pass the test of trials by understanding our trials accomplish God's purpose.**
> **We pass the test of trials by allowing our trials to teach us God's prayer.**
> **We pass the test of trials by letting our trials lead us to God's place.**
> **We pass the test of trials by remembering our trials have God's promise.**

James' commencement address tells us: *"Don't just listen to these six principles and cram them in your heads to know for the test of trials. Learn them until they are a part of who you are, continuing to do them until your faith is your own and your lives take on the qualities of Jesus Christ."* The principle from James' commencement address is *"**Do what the Word says!**"*

The Commencement Address of a Poem

Corrie ten Boom (15 April 1892 – 15 April 1983) was a believer who, along with her father and family members, ran a watch store in the town of Haarlem, Netherlands. The ten Boom family helped many Jews escape German persecution during World War II. In Corrie's bedroom, they built a fake wall creating a special closet in order to hide Jews. This closet became known as *The Hiding Place*. Corrie's father, Casper ten Boom's strong conviction that the Jews were God's chosen people is expressed by his statement, "In this household, God's people are always welcome." A Dutch informant relayed information to the Nazis that the ten Booms were harboring Jews, which was forbidden. Subsequently, they were arrested on February 28, 1944.

Good news and bad news followed their arrest. The bad news was that Casper passed away ten days after his imprisonment. The good news was sent in a letter to Corrie, "All the watches in your cabinet are safe." This was a coded message to communicate that the six individuals who were in *"the hiding place"* during the raid were not discovered but escaped safely.

Corrie and her sister Betsie eventually were transferred to a women's labor camp in Germany, the infamous **Ravensbrück concentration camp. While at this camp,** Betsie's health deteriorated, and she passed away on December 16, 1944. However, before Betsie died she told Corrie, *"There is no pit so deep that He [God] is not deeper still."* Again, there was good news and bad news. With these words fresh on her mind, the good news was delivered fifteen days later when Corrie's was given her freedom. The bad news came later that week at the camp; all the women in Corrie's age group were sent to the gas chambers, where their lives were snuffed out. At a later date, Corrie received information that her release was due to a clerical error, but we know there are no clerical errors, as God is continually working in our lives.

After experiencing this unimaginable trial, Corrie spent the remainder of her life writing books and traveling the world to speak on forgiveness and reconciliation. She even encountered some of the guards from Ravensbrück to which she offered forgiveness. Admittedly, this was not easy for Corrie ten Boom.

When I was in the Netherlands, I had the awesome opportunity to go to the ten Boom watch shop and see *The Hiding Place* for myself. At the end of the tour, our group gathered in the same kitchen where Corrie, her family, and the individuals they hid ate their meals. Though I was familiar with Corrie's life, I was not familiar with the story our tour guide related to us. As Corrie travelled the world speaking to a great number of people, she would take a woven tapestry with her. Our guide held up a framed canvas with a handwoven embroidered picture, but oddly she showed us the backside of the tapestry. The different color threads all ran in a haphazard, disorderly manner

> *"On earth, the underside of the tapestry was tangled and unclear; but in heaven, we will stand amazed to see the topside of the tapestry and how God beautifully embroidered each circumstance into a pattern for our good and His glory."*
>
> -Joni Eareckson Tada
> *Heaven Your Real Home*[1]

creating a confusing mess. At this point our tour guide explained, as Corrie spoke of her life, forgiveness, trials, and challenges she would hold up this very tapestry in the manner in which we were looking at it, from the back side of the canvas. Then she would quote the following poem:

> **My life is but a weaving,**
> **Between my God and me.**
> **I do not choose the colours,**
> **He works so steadily.**
>
> **Oft' times He weaveth sorrow,**
> **And I in foolish pride,**
> **Forget He sees the upper,**
> **And I the underside.**
>
> **Not 'til the loom is silent,**
> **And the shuttles cease to fly,**
> **Will God unroll the canvas,**
> **And reveal the reason why.**
>
> **The dark threads are as needful,**
> **In the Weaver's skillful hand,**
> **As the threads of gold and silver,**
> **In the pattern He has planned.**[2]

At this point, Corrie (and our guide) turned the tapestry around to reveal a beautifully embroidered crown. Ironically, this makes me think of the crown of life James speaks about, and it is an incredible illustration of what God is doing in each of our lives through the testing of our faith. Though from this side it may seem like our lives are an utter mess, God is on the top side making us into an amazing picture of His Son Jesus Christ.

Corrie ten Boom's commencement address to us is the same she poem she gave all over the world: **"The Divine Weaver!"**

The Commencement Address of Power

As we begin to face the challenges of life in a new way, let us gather together one more time to hear our last commencement speaker. The Apostle Paul, who was no stranger to trials, gives our Commencement Address in Romans 8:31-39. In the middle of his address, Paul tells us: *"We are more than conquerors through him who loved us."* "More than conquerors" means we have abundantly more than we need to be victorious because of Jesus' love for us. Read Paul's charge to us, which has the thread of Jesus' marvelous love running throughout it. Read it with the wide-eyed wonder of a child seeing falling snow for the first time.

> What, then, shall we say in response to these things? If God is for us, who can be against us? He who did not spare his own Son, but gave him up for us all—how will he not also, along with him, graciously give us all things? Who will bring any charge against those whom God has chosen? It is God who justifies. Who then is the one who condemns? No one. Christ Jesus who died—more than that, who was raised to life—is at the right hand of God and is also interceding for us. Who shall separate us from the love of Christ? Shall trouble or hardship or persecution or famine or nakedness or danger or sword? As it is written: "For your sake we face death all day long; we are considered as sheep to be slaughtered." **No, in all these things we are more than conquerors through him who loved us.** For I am convinced that neither death nor life, neither angels nor demons, neither the present nor the future, nor any powers, neither height nor depth, nor anything else in all creation, will be able to separate us from the love of God that is in Christ Jesus our Lord. (Romans 8:31-39)

The commencement address of power is **"We are more than conquerors!"**

The Commencement Address for us is to begin *Overcoming Life's Challenges* because we have more than we need to conquer them through the love of Jesus Christ.

THE COMMENCEMENT ADDRESS
-Think About It & Talk About It-

1. Describe a commencement ceremony in which you participated. How was that ceremony the beginning of a new chapter in your life?

2. Below are the six ways James gives us to pass the test of trials.
   a. Briefly, put each one in your own words.
   b. Put a circle around the one Jesus wants you to make a conscious effort to work on this week.
   c. Put a star by the one Jesus wants you to share with another person this week.
   d. Put an arrow by the one Jesus wants you to pray about each day this week.

We pass the test of trials by yielding our trials to God's power.

We pass the test of trials by seeing our trials from God's perspective.

We pass the test of trials by understanding our trials accomplish God's purpose.

We pass the test of trials by allowing our trials to teach us God's prayer.

We pass the test of trials by letting our trials lead us to God's place.

We pass the test of trials by remembering our trials have God's promise.

3. How does Corrie ten Boom's life model the principles James gives us?

4. How could you use the poem *"Life Is But a Weaving"* to help a friend as he or she is going through the test of trials?

5. Reflect on your current trials. How does Romans 8:31-39 encourage you? When it comes to *Overcoming Life's Challenges,* what does it mean to you that you are *"more than a conqueror through him who loved you?"*

The End

THE STUFF

@

THE END

"Everything before Jesus is preface.
Everything after Jesus is appendix.
Jesus is the story."

-Kevin DeYoung, Author

APPENDIX A:
A Closer Look @ The Life of James

James was Jesus' earthly half-brother. Matthew 13:53-58

*When Jesus had finished these parables, he moved on from there. Coming to his hometown, he began teaching the people in their synagogue, and they were amazed. "Where did this man get this wisdom and these miraculous powers?" they asked. "Isn't this the carpenter's son? Isn't his mother's name Mary, and **aren't his brothers James**, Joseph, Simon and Judas? Aren't all his sisters with us? Where then did this man get all these things?" And they took offense at him. But Jesus said to them, "A prophet is not without honor except in his own town and in his own home." And he did not do many miracles there because of their lack of faith. [cm Mark 6:1-6; Matt. 12:46-47; Mark 3:31-35; Luke 8:19-21; John 2:12]*

1. Matthew and Mark place James first in their list of Jesus' siblings, implying that he was the eldest of the half-brothers.

2. Matthew and Mark both note another half-brother of Jesus and brother to James. He is listed as Judas, but we are more familiar with him as Jude. Jude was also used by God to be the human author of a book of the Bible that bears his name. Jude 1:1a reads, *"Jude, a servant of Jesus Christ and a brother of James."* Note the similarity of Jude and James' description of themselves: *"a servant (doulos) of Jesus Christ."*

3. Surely James was influenced by the Sermon on the Mount, because many of its themes have parallels in his epistle. Undoubtedly, James heard the truths of the Sermon on the Mount from Jesus and may have heard the sermon firsthand.

James was a believer later in life. Mark 3:21; John 7:5

When his family heard about this, they went to take charge of him, for they said, "He [Jesus] is out of his mind." (Mark 3:21)

For even his [Jesus] own brothers did not believe in him. (John 7:5)

1. Jesus family, including James, thought He was crazy, a lunatic, gone mad. Imagine if your brother stated that He was God and was going to die for the sin of the world. You would probably think he was out of His mind, too. Charles Swindoll makes this comment on Mark 3:21, "The Living Bible says, 'He's out of His mind.' The Berkeley says, 'He is deranged.' Phillips' New Testament says, "He must be mad.' The decided opinion of the family, apparently including James, was, 'He's a nut!' John 7:5 says, 'For not even His brothers were believing in Him.'"[1]

2. Their unbelief probably lasted throughout most, if not all of Jesus' earthly life. We note a very telling scene at the cross. Jesus entrusted His mother Mary to the Apostle John and not any family members. Apparently, they still were not followers of Jesus.

> *Near the cross of Jesus stood his mother, his mother's sister, Mary the wife of Clopas, and Mary Magdalene. When Jesus saw his mother there, and **the disciple whom he loved** standing nearby, he said to her, "Woman, here is your son," and to the disciple, "Here is your mother." From that time on, this disciple took her into his home. (John 19:25-27)*

James was one that saw the resurrected Christ. 1 Corinthians 15:3-8; Acts 1:12-14

1. The resurrection changed James.

   *For what I received I passed on to you as of first importance: that Christ died for our sins according to the Scriptures, that he was buried, that he was raised on the third day according to the Scriptures, and that he appeared to Cephas, and then to the Twelve. After that, he appeared to more than five hundred of the brothers and sisters at the same time, most of whom are still living, though some have fallen asleep. **Then he appeared to James,** then to all the apostles, and last of all he appeared to me also, as to one abnormally born.* (1Corinthians 15:3-8)

2. James' possible timeline: James is not mentioned at the cross which might lean toward the fact that he was still an unbeliever or a fairly new believer. From 1 Corinthians 15, we note, James saw the resurrected Christ. Had James put his trust in Jesus before or did the resurrection bring him to a point of belief? This is not clear. In Acts 1:12-14, we find Mary the mother of Jesus and His brothers meeting with the apostles. This is sometime between the ascension (Acts 1:9-11) and the Day of Pentecost (Acts 2:1-41). We can say with certainty that James had been changed from a skeptic that thought Jesus a lunatic to a devoted follower, at least by this time between the resurrection and the Day of Pentecost.

   Then the apostles returned to Jerusalem from the hill called the Mount of Olives, a Sabbath day's walk from the city. When they arrived, they went upstairs to the room where they were staying. Those present were Peter, John, James and Andrew; Philip and Thomas, Bartholomew and Matthew;

James son of Alphaeus and Simon the Zealot, and Judas son of James. They all joined together constantly in prayer, **along with the women and Mary the mother of Jesus, and with his brothers.** (Acts 1:12-14)

James was an intrical part of the early church in Jerusalem.

1. James was a "Pastor," probably the "Senior Pastor," of the church at Jerusalem. (Acts 12:17; 21:17-19; Galatians 1:18-20)

   Peter motioned with his hand for them to be quiet and described how the Lord had brought him out of prison. "Tell **James** *and the other brothers and sisters about this," he said, and then he left for another place.* (Acts 12:17)

   When we arrived at Jerusalem, the brothers and sisters received us warmly. The next day Paul and the rest of us went to see **James, and all the elders were present.** *Paul greeted them and reported in detail what God had done among the Gentiles through his ministry.* (Acts 21:17-19)

   *Then after three years, I went up to Jerusalem to get acquainted with Cephas and stayed with him fifteen days. I saw none of the other apostles—***only James, the Lord's brother.** *I assure you before God that what I am writing you is no lie.* (Galatians 1:18-20)

2. James was a "Pillar" of the early church. (Galatians 2:9-12)

   James, *Cephas and John, those esteemed as pillars, gave me and Barnabas the right hand of fellowship when they recognized the grace given to me. They agreed that we should go to the Gentiles, and they to the circumcised. All they asked was that we should continue to remember the poor, the very thing I had been eager to do all along. When Cephas came to Antioch, I opposed him to his face, because he stood condemned. For before certain men came from* **James,** *he used to eat with the Gentiles. But when they* *arrived, he began to draw back and separate himself from the Gentiles because he was afraid of those who belonged to the circumcision group.* (Galatians 2:9-12)

3. James was "Moderator" over the Jerusalem Council deciding how to handle the new Gentile believers. (Acts 15:6-29)

James was a man of prayer, according to Christian tradition.

1. James was known as "James the Just." Because of James's faithfulness to the law and his devotion to prayer, he was called "James the Just." "James became a respected and beloved figure in the early church, especially among Jewish Christians. He was considered the first 'bishop' of the Jerusalem church and was called the 'righteous' or the 'just' because of his faithfulness to the law and his devotion to prayer."[2]

2. James was known as "Camel Knees." "It was the nickname that the early church gave to the writer of this Epistle. It is said that his knees were as hard as camel's knees; and the reason for that is not far to seek - he was a great man of prayer, and was so constantly on his knees that they had worn hard!"[3]

James was a martyr, according to Christian tradition.[4]

1. There is mention of James' death in the Scriptures, but tradition tells us he was martyred in A.D. 62. The Jewish historian Josephus in his writing *Antiquities* 20.200-201, also gives us indication that James' death occurred in A.D. 62.

2. It is said that the Pharisees in Jerusalem so despised James' testimony form Christ that they had him thrown down from the temple and beaten with clubs.

3. It is reported that James died, as did Jesus, by praying, "Father, forgive them, for they know not what they do."

4. Hegesippus, an early second-century Christian, describes James's death in his *Memoirs*. He claimed that James was stoned to death by the scribes and Pharisees for refusing to renounce his commitment to Jesus (Eusebius, *History of the Church* 2.23).

5. In his writing Antiquities 20-2000-201, affirms the essentials of James' story.

APPENDIX B:
A Closer Look @ The Tests of James

In order to better establish a foundation for *Overcoming Life's Challenges* and a connection to James' letter, the author's understanding of James' epistle is discussed in this appendix. It has been said that the book of James does not lend itself to a nice outline. James tends to be brief in his discussion of topics, circles around, and touches on them again. It has even been suggested that the book of James is snippets of sermons he delivered. One can find a number of outlines or ways of viewing James' letter which have commonality.

James message is: if we have genuine faith in Jesus Christ, our faith will be evident by a change in the way we live our lives. The author proposes that James presents a series of tests to demonstrate and develop one's faith. The testing of our faith will examine: 1) what an individual believes and, 2) what that faith will look like as he or she lives it out. This is why James' letter is so practical and convicting. A couple of passages will be considered to assist in leading us to this conclusion.

James 1:2-3, *"Consider it pure joy, my brothers, whenever you face trials of many kinds,* **because you know that the testing of your faith** *produces perseverance."* James begins his letter by telling us that the testing of our faith will come and we are confident it is accomplishing its work. As noted in chapter 3, *"When will I ever Use This In Real Life?"* the word for testing is "to prove something is genuine". Throughout his book, James outlines a series of tests to be used to demonstrate an individual's faith is genuine. These tests also are used to develop one's faith into mature. A maturity that reflects Jesus Christ.

James 2:18, *"But someone will say, "You have faith; I have deeds." Show me your faith without deeds, and **I will show you my faith by my deeds**."* James is not saying that we have to perform good works or "deeds" for our salvation but that genuine saving faith will produce good deeds as an evidence of one's salvation. It must be noted, James is not suggesting that the believer will always scores 100% on each test of faith but James is describing the characteristics, tendencies, and direction of a genuine believer's life.

Each of these tests should cause us to pause and ask ourselves if we are genuine believers. 2 Corinthians 13:5 gives clear instructions for this self-evaluation: *Examine yourselves to see whether you are in the faith; test yourselves. Do you not realize that Christ Jesus is in you—unless, of course, you fail the test?*

Each of these tests should cause us to pause and ask ourselves if we are doers of the Word. James 1:22 (NLT) puts it this way, *But don't just listen to God's word. You must do what it says. Otherwise, you are only fooling yourselves.*

This is the author's understanding of how James' testing demonstrates and develops our faith.

- ❖ The Test of **Trials;** James 1:1-12

- ❖ The Test of **Temptation;** James 1:13-19

- ❖ The Test of the **Word;** James 1:19-27

- ❖ The Test of **Love;** James 2:1-13

- ❖ The Test of the **Faith;** James 2:14-20

- ❖ The Test of the **Tongue;** James 3:1-12

- ❖ The Test of **Wisdom;** James 3:13-18

- ❖ The Test of **Submission;** James 4:1-17

- ❖ The Test of **Wealth;** James 5:1-6

- ❖ The Test of **Patience;** James 5:7-11

- ❖ The Test of **Prayer;** James 5:12-18

- ❖ The Test of **Restoration;** James 5:19-20

APPENDIX C:
A Closer Look @ the Greek Word for Trials
[πειρασμος - *peirasmos*]

A General Look @ Test or Trial [πειρ - *peir*]

As noted in chapter two, *"But I experience Test Anxiety!"* the general root for trial is *peir* and means "test." The simple definition is "a trial is a test". [Both *peirasmos* meaning trial in James 1:2, 12 and *peirazo* meaning temptation in James 1:13-14 have this same root.] Greek scholars Louw and Nida give us the following discussion on the general meaning of *peir*: "to try to learn the nature or character of someone or something by submitting such to thorough and extensive testing - 'to test, to examine, to put to test, examination, testing'". They continue by adding: "to obtain information to be used against a person by trying to cause someone to make a mistake - 'to try to trap, to attempt to catch in a mistake'". An example used to aid our understanding of *peir* is how the Pharisees and Sadducees continually tried to trap or catch Jesus in a mistake.[1]

A Specific Look @ Test or Trial [πειρασμος - *peirasmos*] in James 1:2, 12

James takes the root *peir* and uses the noun form *peirasmos* in James 1:2 and 12. The context of James' discussion makes it clear he is discussing the test of trials. The fuller definition of trials used in this book reflects the purpose of trials as seen in James 1:3-4. James gives us two main purposes for trials: 1) God uses tests to prove the authenticity of our faith; 2) God uses tests to develop our spiritual maturity. (These two purposes are covered to a greater degree in chapter three, *"When Will I Ever Use This in Real Life?"*). The definition used for this book and derived from James' usage is: *A trial is a test God uses to prove the genuineness of our faith and to develop our maturity in Jesus Christ.*

A Specific Look @ Temptation [πειραζω - *peirazo*] in James 1:13-14

James 1:13-14 tells us, *When tempted, no one should say, "God is tempting me." For God cannot be tempted by evil, nor does he tempt anyone; but each person is tempted when they are dragged away by their own evil desire and enticed.*

As noted, James uses the noun form, *peirasmos,* which is translated trials in James 1:2, 12. In James 1:13-14, he uses the same root word, *peri*-test, but now James uses the verb form *peirazo,* and it is translated temptation. Though the root is the same, the concept is different, and James' discussion in James 1:13-15 is now about the test of temptation. Again, we draw on the meaning of our root word *peir* and the usage of the word by James in these verses to determine what James means. With that in mind, we offer this definition: *A temptation is an inner desire that seeks to induce sin and to hinder the development of our faith.*

Clearly in verse 13, James tells us God is not responsible for tempting us to sin. In verse 14, James states: the temptation to sin comes from our own evil desires. In case that is not enough, James takes us another step by using this same Greek root word *peir* to describe God. God cannot be tempted by evil. The Greek word is *aperiasmos.* When we separate the word into its parts, "*a*" meaning "not" and "*periasmos*" meaning "temptation," we discover this about *aperiasmos*: "not able to be tempted, 'invincible to assault of evils.'"[2] Sin is not a part of God's character. In fact sin is the opposite of His character, and it does not even appeal to Him. A couple of comments will help in our understanding of God's part in trials and non-participation in temptations: "But while God may test or prove his servants in order to strengthen their faith, He never seeks to induce sin and destroy their faith. Thus, despite the fact that the same Greek root (*peira-*) is used for both the outer trial and the inner temptation, it is crucial to distinguish them."[3] "'What must be understood is that temptation is an impulse to sin, and since God is not susceptible to any such desire for evil He cannot be seen as desiring that it be brought about in man.'"[4]

A Concluding Look @ Trials and Temptations

When James originally wrote his letter, there were no verses markings and no chapter divisions. In his simple and straightforward manner, James moves from trials in verses 2-12 to temptation in verses 13-18. This is where it is paramount we remember that the context is key. The context and how James is using the word determines our meaning. Much like we would determine the meaning of the word trunk by the context of its usage e.g. "The elephant used his trunk to put peanuts in his mouth." "During the snow season, I keep a shovel, a bag of sand, and boots in the trunk of my car." "We were going to the pool, so I grab my swimming trunks."

In James 1:2-12, the context is clear that James' discussion focuses on how God is actively involved in the test of trials in order to prove our faith and develop perseverance and spiritual maturity in us. In James 1:13-18, the context is clear that James' discussion focuses on how our own evil desires are actively involved in the test of temptations that lead to sin and death.

The purpose of this appendix is to give clarity to the issue and relationship of trials and temptations. It is not intended to be an exhaustive look at all the implications of this issue. It is recognized that other passages and questions certainly will come to mind regarding trials and temptations. The appendix is also to serve as a springboard for our understanding and further study of God's Word regarding the important issues of trials and temptations.

NOTES @ THE END

A NOTE FROM A FELLOW BEGGAR
[1]Derick Bingham, Encouragement – Oxygen for the Soul (Christian Focus, 1997), 54.

Intro - NEXT EXIT: THE SCHOOL OF HARD KNOCKS
[1]http://www.sheknows.com/living/articles/1023453/what-are-the-odds-21-statistics-that-will-surprise-you [assessed fall of 2017]. This website also noted by * in the introduction.

[2]http://www.funny2.com/odds.htm [assessed fall of 2017]. This website also noted by # in the introduction.

[3]A more detailed description of James is given in **Appendix A: A Closer Look @ The Life of James.**[4]Charles Swindoll, James: Practical and Authentic Living, *Bible Study Guide* (Fullerton, CA: Insight For Living, 1991), 2-3. Charles Swindoll makes this comment on Mark 3:21: "The Living Bible says, 'He's out of His mind.' The Berkeley says, 'He is deranged.' Phillips' New Testament says, "He must be mad.' The decided opinion of the family, apparently including James, was, 'He's a nut!' John 7:5 says, 'For not even His brothers were believing in Him.'"

[5]Gary R. Mayes, Now What (Wheaton, IL: Crossway Books, 1995), 143.

[6]James Montgomery Boice, The Minor Prophets: Two Volumes Complete in One Edition (Grand Rapids, MI: Kregel Publications, 1983, 1986), 1:218.

[7]The author's understanding of the foundation of the book of James and how the tests of James unfold are given in **Appendix B: A Closer Look @ The Tests of James.**

Chapter 1 - MY TEACHER DOESN'T LIKE ME!
[1]Douglas J. Moo, The Letter of James: *The Pillar New Testament Commentary* (Grand Rapids: Eerdmans, 2000), 6. "Absent from James are the customary greetings, references to fellow workers, and travel plans that mark many ancient and NT (especially Pauline) letters. Also missing are references to specific

people, places, or situations in the body of the letter. Where James does refer to a situation, he casts it in a vague, even hypothetical manner (e.g., 2:2-3, 15-17; 4:13-17)."

[2]J. Gresham Machen, New Testament Greek for Beginners (New York: The MacMillian Co., 1961), 57. "The vocative case is the case of direct address." Machen p.25

[3]I want to express my appreciation for insights from Pastor Ryland Walter's sermon "The Heart of a Servant," preached at Rock Brook Church; September 2-3, 2017. Used by permission.

[4]Henry T. Blackaby and Claude V. King, Experiencing God, (Nashville, TN: Broadman & Holman Publishers, 1994), 25.

[5]Spiros Zodhiates, The Behavior of Belief (Grand Rapids, MI: Eerdmans Publishing Co., 1959), 18. "This is what is call the diaspora of the twelve tribes. It is the scattering of persecuted Jerusalem believers. But is it merely a scattering for their safety? Remember that God permits persecution and hardship in the believer's life always to accomplish some higher purpose. And there is no higher purpose either with God or with God's children than the salvation of precious souls through the sowing of the seed of the Gospel of Jesus Christ."

[6]A.W. Tozer, The Root of the Righteous, (Chicago, IL: Moody Publishers).

[7]I have heard various details of the account of Thomas Haukes' story and have put them together here. This account was taken from Fox's Book of Martyrs, http://graceonlinelibrary.org/biographies/the-martyrdom-of-thomas-haukes-by-john-fox/ [accessed 10/05/2017].

Chapter 2 - BUT I EXPERIENCE TEST ANXIETY!

[1]F. Michael Grubbs, Top Down Thinking in a Bottom Up World (Unpublished work), 2017.

[2]"Ten Ways to Overcome Test Anxiety," https://www.princetonreview.com/college-advice/test-anxiety [accessed 12/20/17].

[3]Machen, New Testament Greek for Beginners, 57. Middle Voice – "The middle voice represents the subject as acting in some way that concerns itself, or as acting upon something that belongs to itself."

[4]A more thorough discussion is given in **APPENDIX C: A Closer Look @ the Greek Word for Trial** [πειρασμος - *peirasmos*].

[5]Louw and Nida, Greek Scholars: Greek-English Lexicon Based on Semantic Domain. Copyright © 1988 United Bible Societies, New York. Used by permission.

[6]Zodhiates, The Behavior of Belief, 22. Emphasis added

[7]Swindoll, James: Practical and Authentic Living, *Bible Study Guide*, 17.

Chapter 3 - WHEN WILL I EVER USE THIS IN REAL LIFE?

[1]Joseph Stowell, Fan the Flame: Living Out Your First Love for Christ (Chicago, IL: Moody Publishers, 1986), 32.

[2]Comments from Dave Kennedy mathematics instructor for over 40 years at both the high school and university level

[3]This definition is by Greek Scholar W.E. Vine from his complete works set. The remainder of the definition and observations come from the author's study of that Greek word.

[4]Fritz Rienecker and Cleon L. Rogers, Jr., A Linguistic Key to the Greek New Testament (Grand Rapids, MI: The Zondervan Corporation, Regency Reference Library, 1980), 721.

[5]Moo, The Letter of James: *The Pillar New Testament Commentary,* 54-55.

[6]Ibid., 55.

[7]Zodhiates, The Behavior of Belief, 26.

[8]Phillips Brooks (12/13/1835 - 1/23/1893) was an American clergyman, author, and most notably remembered as lyricist of the Christmas hymn, "O Little Town of Bethlehem," in 1868.

[9]http://kushandwizdom.tumblr.com/

[10]Moo, The Letter of James: *The Pillar New Testament Commentary,* 56. "...*teleios* is colored by its Hebrew background and come to mean 'complete' or 'mature.'"

[11]Rienecker and Rogers, Jr., A Linguistic Key to the Greek New Testament, 721.

[12]https://www.runnersworld.com/runners-stories/dead-freakin-lastand-proud-of-it.

Chapter 4 - ISN'T THE LEARNING CENTER FOR DUMMIES?

[1]Mayes, Now What, 49.

[2]Quote attributed to Charles H. Spurgeon in a number of sites, but the author was unable to find the original source. Charles Haddon Spurgeon (19 June 1834 – 31 January 1892) was an English Particular Baptist preacher. He is known as the "Prince of Preachers." Spurgeon was the pastor of the New Park Street Chapel, later known as the Metropolitan Tabernacle, in London for 38 years. Through books, sermons, and quotes, he still remains highly influential today.

[3]Mayes, Now What!, 159.

[4]John MacArthur Jr. James: The MacArthur New Testament Commentary (Chicago: Moody Press, 1998), 36.

[5]Rienecker and Rogers, A Linguistic Key to the Greek New Testament, 721.

[6]Ibid.

[7]MacArthur, James: The MacArthur New Testament Commentary, 36.

[8]Alexander Maclaren (11 February 1826 – 5 May 1910) was an English non-conformist Baptist minister of Scottish origin. He ministered for 45 years in the mill city of Manchester, England. He was a contemporary of other prominent preachers, such as Charles H. Spurgeon, Joseph Parker, and F. B. Meyer. He was known as "the prince of expositors."

[9]Rienecker and Rogers, A Linguistic Key to the Greek New Testament, 722.

[10]Moo, The Letter of James: The Pillar New Testament Commentary, 61.

[11]Zodhiates, The Behavior of Belief, 40.

[12]Ibid.

[13]"George Müller Quotes, ghttps://www.goodreads.com/quotes/1188294-the-greater-the-difficulty-to-be-overcome-the-more-will [accessed 12/20/17].

[14] George Müller, "The Autobiography of George Muller, (Whitaker House, 1984), 152-153.

Chapter 5 - DOESN'T MY TEACHER GRADE ON A CURVE?

[1]C.S. Lewis, Mere Christianity, (C.S. Lewis Pte. Ltd. ©1952, renewed ©1980).

[2]Dr. Seuss, Oh the Places We Go, (Random House, 1990).

[3]Rienecker and Rogers, A Linguistic Key to the Greek New Testament, 722.

[4]Ibid.

[5]Moo, The Letter of James: The Pillar New Testament Commentary, 65.

[6]Ibid., 66.

[7]The account can be read in its entirety in Luke 18:18-30.

[8]C.S. Lewis, Mere Christianity.

[9]Rienecker and Rogers, A Linguistic Key to the Greek New Testament, 722.

[10]Ibid., 723.

Chapter 6 - I'M BEING RECOGNIZED AT THE AWARDS' CEREMONY!?

[1]Randy Alcorn, The Treasure Principle, (Eternal Perspective Ministries: 2002), 39.

[2]MacArthur, James: The MacArthur New Testament Commentary, 41.

[3]Rienecker and Rogers, A Linguistic Key to the Greek New Testament, 794.

Summary – THE COMMENCEMENT ADDRESS

[1]Joni Eareckson Tada, Heaven: Your Real Home (Zondervan Publishing, 1995), 44-45.

[2]"The Divine Weaver" (the Tapestry Poem) attributed to Corrie ten Boom but probable the author is Grant Colfax Tuller.

Appendix A – A CLOSER LOOK @ THE LIFE OF JAMES

[1]Swindoll, James: Practical and Authentic Living, Bible Study Guide, 2-3.

[2]Moo, The Letter of James: The Pillar New Testament Commentary, 16.

[3]Guy King, A Belief That Behaves (Fort Washington, PA: Christian Literature Crusade, 1974), 119.

[4]Information for "**James was a martyr, according to Christian tradition**" drawn from two sources: Warren Wiersbe, James: The Bible Exposition Commentary Two Volumes (Colorado Springs, CO: Victor Books, 1989), 2:334 and Moo, The Letter of James: The Pillar New Testament Commentary, 16.

Appendix C – A CLOSER LOOK @ THE GREEK WORD FOR TRIALS [*peirasmos*]

[1]Louw and Nida, Greek Scholars: Greek-English Lexicon Based on Semantic Domain. Copyright © 1988 United Bible Societies, New York. Used by permission.

[2]Rienecker and Rogers, A Linguistic Key to the Greek New Testament, 723.

[3]Moo, The Letter of James: The Pillar New Testament Commentary, 73.

[4]Ibid., 74.   Moo quoting S. Laws, A Commentary on the Epistle of James (New York: Harper & Row, 1980), 71.

ACKNOWLEDGEMENTS

Thanks to....

Sarah Buchan for help in capturing the concept for the cover and into a visual reality. www.sarahbuchanphotography.com

Tara Dunn for her assistance on the interior formatting.

Dr. Jerrod Fellhauer for his insight on test anxiety and website information.

Mike Grubbs for saying, "If God wants you to write, sit down and write!"

Dave Kennedy for assistance in writing the introduction for the "When Will I Ever Use This in Real Life?" chapter by sharing his insight from over 40 years of teaching.

Dr. Kris Schuler for her eyes of editing, and the encouragement that came with her reviews.

Suzanne Williams, my sister, for volunteering to bring another set of eyes to the manuscript and for her invaluable recommendations.

Noah for letting me bounce ideas off him and for putting together the website.

Josiah for asking, "Dad, why don't you write?"

Micah for guiding my thoughts as we talked about the introduction to the question: "If you were on trial for being a Christian, would there be enough evidence for a jury to convict you?"

Mom and Dad for being the first to read my very, very rough family manuscript, and continually believing in me.

Jenny Wildman for asking when my next book is coming out.

Daisy for training me to give her a treat every time I sat down at the computer.

ABOUT THE AUTHOR

Steve Baird and his wife Lisa have been married for thirty years. They have two college age sons and one high school age son. During those thirty years they have ministered together, with Steve serving as a Youth Pastor, a Senior Pastor, College Instructor, College Administrator, and a minister in a local church. Steve earned a Bachelor's of Arts Degree in Theology and a Master's of Arts Degree in biblical languages.

Steve Baird is a creative and gifted communicator committed to speaking God's unchanging Word to an ever-changing world. God has graciously given him opportunities to pursue his passion of teaching God's Word in a variety of settings. Steve has lead workshops at two National Youth Conventions, been the featured speaker at camps, a guest instructor and commencement speaker at the Nassau Theological College in Tanzania, a regular guest speaker for Campus Crusade, and a co-chaplain for the University of Nebraska at Kearney football team.

Steve Baird is the founder of E710 Ministries, a speaking and writing ministry. The ministry is based on the description of Ezra as told to us in Ezra 7:10 (ESV), *"For Ezra had set his heart to study the Law of the LORD, and to do it and to teach his statutes and rules in Israel."* E710 Ministries exists to assist individuals in encountering the written and living Christ, resulting in life change. E710 Ministries' mission is to dig into the depths of God's Word, to present Jesus Christ in an understandable way, and to allow the Spirit to change lives.

Check out E710 Ministries: e710ministries.com

While you're there, Steve invites you make a comment on this book, discover more about his writings, and inquire about having him speak at your next event.

HOPE TO HEAR FROM YOU!!

OVERCOMING LIFE'S CHALLENGES:
"Do I Need to Know This for the Final?"

At this very moment, each of us finds ourselves going into, in the middle of, or coming out of one of life's challenges. Whether the challenge is mental, emotional, relational, physical or spiritual, we experience the testing of our faith daily. God's desire for us is to not merely pass the test but to demonstrate our faith is genuine and develop the character of Jesus Christ. As we attend the school of hard knocks together, lets us learn principles from James that will enable us to Overcome Life's Challenges!

Overcoming Life's Challenges: Do I Need to Know This for the Final? is the book that provides the foundation and background for the eight session *Overcoming Life's Challenges Participant's Guide* and DVD.

"I have greatly enjoyed working through Steve Baird's "Overcoming Life's Challenges" with my men's small group. We found the book to be insightful and helpful in guiding our examination of the scriptural basis for the trials in our lives. I heartily recommend this book both for personal study and for small group use."

Kelly Walter | Founding Pastor
Rock Brook Church

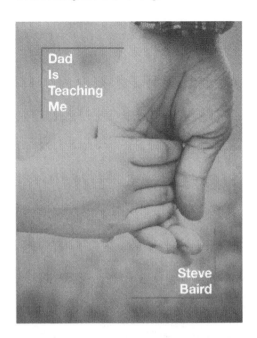

DAD IS TEACHING ME IS FOR YOU!!

Whether you are a man, a woman, a boy, or a girl, this booklet is a gift to YOU!! From the beginning to the end, you will unwrap timeless principles revealing the heart of our *Heavenly Father*. In His unmeasurable wisdom, our Heavenly Father has designed *Earthly Fathers* to be a visible representation of Him and to be instrumental in writing their children's stories. Sprinkled throughout this gift, you find children sharing their stories of what their *Earthly Fathers* taught them. This booklet guides *Earthly Fathers* to become men of God and provides them with useful steps to instruct their children in the Lord. As you remove the gift wrapping from each lesson in *Dad Is Teaching Me,* learn from an *Earthly Father* whose life says, *"My son, give me your heart, and let your eyes keep to my ways"* (Proverb 23:26).

"WOW! That is an incredible devotional. I was ministered to while reading it. You have picked out some key topics and written so well. Hats off to you and May God cause Dads to be better followers and imitators of Christ."   *-Clay, father of 3 sons*

COMING SOON

NAVIGATING LIFE'S MAZE
Following Abraham's Steps to the Will of God

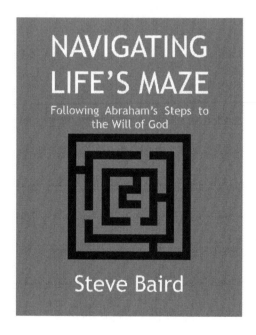

(Not final cover)

We hope to finally turn that corner in life which will be a clear path to God's will for us. In reality, we turn that corner only to find a wall, and another turn. Life can be is like a maze, so how do we navigate it? At times we feel God is hiding His will, but He wants us to know and do His will more than we do. Let's travel back to a time when God navigated Abraham through the maze of his life. *"Leave your country, your people and your father's household and go to the land I will show you"* (Genesis 12:1). As we follow Abraham's footsteps, we discover timeless principles that God uses to guide each of us through Life's Maze!

Made in the USA
Columbia, SC
24 April 2019